W9-AMI-452

The 20th Century's
MOST INFLUENTIAL
HISPANICS

Che Guevara
Revolutionary

by Michael V. Uschan

LUCENT BOOKS
An imprint of Thomson Gale, a part of The Thomson Corporation

THOMSON
™
GALE

Detroit • New York • San Francisco • New Haven, Conn. • Waterville, Maine • London

THOMSON

━━━━━✳━━━━━ ™

GALE

Dedico este libro con amor a Juan Carlos Castañeda Rojas y Juan Carlos Charum Monzón.

© 2007 Thomson Gale, a part of The Thomson Corporation.
Thomson and Star Logo are trademarks and Gale and Lucent Books are registered trademarks used herein under license.

For more information, contact
Lucent Books
27500 Drake Rd.
Farmington Hills, MI 48331-3535
Or you can visit our Internet site at http://www.gale.com

ALL RIGHTS RESERVED.
No part of this work covered by the copyright hereon may be reproduced or used in any form or by any means—graphic, electronic, or mechanical, including photocopying, recording, taping, Web distribution, or information storage retrieval systems—without the written permission of the publisher. Every effort has been made to trace the owners of copyrighted material.

LIBRARY OF CONGRESS CATALOGING-IN-PUBLICATION DATA

Uschan, Michael V., 1948–
  Che Guevara, revolutionary / by Michael V. Uschan.
    p. cm.— (Twentieth century's most influential Hispanics)
  Includes bibliographical references and index.
  ISBN 13: 978-1-59018-970-2 (hardcover : alk. paper)
  ISBN10: 1-59018-970-1 (hardcover : alk. paper)
  1. Guevara, Ernesto, 1928-1967—Juvenile literature. 2. Cuba—History—1959—Juvenile literature. 3. Latin America—History—1948–1980—Juvenile literature. 4. Guerrillas—Latin America—Biography—Juvenile literature. I. Title. II. Series.
  F2849.22.G85U83 2006
  980.03'5092—dc22

                                                           2006016801

Printed in the United States of America

Table of Contents

Foreword

When Alberto Gonzales was a boy living in Texas, he never dreamed he would one day stand next to the president of the United States. Born to poor migrant workers, Gonzales grew up in a two-bedroom house shared by his family of ten. There was no telephone or hot water. Because his parents were too poor to send him to college, Gonzales joined the Air Force, but after two years was able to transfer to Rice University. College was still a time of struggle for Gonzales, who had to sell refreshments in the bleachers during football games to support himself. But he eventually went on to Harvard Law School and rose to prominence in the Texas government. Then one day, decades after rising from his humble beginnings in Texas, he found himself standing next to President George W. Bush at the White House. The president had nominated him to be the nation's first Hispanic attorney general. As he accepted the nomination, Gonzales embraced the president and said, "'Just give me a chance to prove myself'—that is a common prayer for those in my community. Mr. President, thank you for that chance."

Like Gonzales, many Hispanics in the United States and elsewhere have shed humble beginnings to soar to impressive and previously unreachable heights. In the twenty-first century, influential Hispanic figures can be found worldwide and in all fields of endeavor, including science, politics, education, the arts, sports, religion, and literature. Some accomplishments, like those of musician Carlos Santana or author Alisa Valdes-Rodriguez, have added a much-needed Hispanic voice to the artistic landscape. Others, such as revolutionary Che Guevara or labor leader Dolores Huerta, have spawned international social movements that have enriched the rights of all peoples.

In America, Hispanics are reaching new heights of cultural influence, buying power, and political clout. More than 35 million people identified themselves as Hispanic on the 2000 U.S. census, and there were estimated to be more than 41 million Hispanics in America as of 2006. In the twenty-first century people of Hispanic origin have officially become the nation's largest ethnic minority, outnumbering both blacks and Asians. Hispanics constitute about 13 percent of the nation's total population, and by 2050 their numbers are expected to rise to 102.6 million, at which point they would account for 24 percent of the total population. With growing numbers and expanding influence, Hispanic leaders, artists, politicians, and scientists in America and in other countries are commanding attention like never before.

These unique and fascinating stories are the subjects of The Twentieth Century's Most Influential Hispanics collection from Lucent Books. Each volume in the series critically examines the challenges, accomplishments, and legacies of influential Hispanic figures; many of whom, like Alberto Gonzales, sprang from modest beginnings to achieve groundbreaking goals. The Twentieth Century's Most Influential Hispanics series offers vivid narrative, fully documented primary and secondary source quotes, bibliography, thorough index, and mix of color and black-and-white photographs, which enhance each volume and provide excellent starting points for research and discussion.

A "Complete Human Being"

On October 9, 1967, Che Guevara was shot to death in Bolivia. Soldiers for the Bolivian army, aided by U.S. Central Intelligence Agency (CIA) operatives, had hunted him down and captured him because he was leading an armed rebellion to overthrow that country's government. Shortly after Guevara's death, French philosopher Jean-Paul Sartre declared that "Che was the most complete human being of our age."[1] That was high praise from someone who was one of the twentieth century's most acclaimed philosophers as well as a noted playwright, novelist, and critic.

Sartre's worshipful tribute acknowledged the many aspects of Guevara's life and personality that were unknown to most people, even those who instantly recognized his name and face. Guevara was famous before his death, but his celebrity had been based almost solely on his having helped Fidel Castro bring Communist rule to Cuba. Guevara had played a key role in overthrowing dictator Fulgencio Batista in 1959 by formulating principles of guerrilla warfare that had enabled the small, ragtag band of Cuban revolutionaries to defeat a much larger, better-equipped military force.

Guevara, however, was much more than an able military strategist and commander. He was a physician and a prolific writer. He authored hundreds of newspaper and magazine articles, numerous poems, and several books, including one on guerrilla warfare that military experts still study today. As a young man, he had also worked as a professional photographer, taking pictures of news and sports events for Latin American newspapers. Guevara was also an economist—he shaped Cuba's new economic structure after Castro seized power—and a political and social philosopher whose views are still respected in parts of the world four decades after his death.

The Latin American Don Quixote

Despite the varied outlets that Guevara discovered for his many talents, he had a much more restricted personal vision of who

Three Cubans pose for a picture before a mosaic of Che Guevara. They are among the millions of people who still revere Guevara today.

he was. Above all else, Guevara considered himself a revolutionary, someone who overthrows governments not just to install new leaders but to establish an entirely new way of governing people. Guevara believed revolutions were necessary when existing governments oppressed the citizens they ruled. Guevara once stated this view of himself in a letter to his family: "I believe in armed struggle as the only solution for the peoples who struggle to free themselves [from oppression], and I act in accordance with my convictions. Many will call me an adventurer and I am, but of a different kind—one who risks his skin to prove their truths."[2]

Guevara's commitment to being a revolutionary was triggered by the poverty, suffering, and injustice he witnessed in Latin America. His revolutionary zeal, however, was tinged by a haze of romanticism that had also been born in his youth.

One of Guevara's favorite novels was *Don Quixote* by Miguel de Cervantes, the classic tale about a deluded old man who wanders through Spain on a horse trying to right injustices, most of them imagined. Like Don Quixote, the book's whimsi-

In a 1961 speech in Uruguay, Che Guevara accuses the United States of plotting to kill Cuban leader Fidel Castro.

cal hero, Guevara viewed himself as someone whose mission in life was to help people. Guevara identified so strongly with Don Quixote that he comically assumed that character in the last letter he wrote to his parents before his death in Bolivia. In early January 1967, Guevara wished his parents well in the coming year: "Through the dust kicked up by the hooves of Rocinante [the horse Quixote rode], with my spear poised to hurl at the enemy giants who are pursuing me, I hurry to send you this almost telepathic message and pass on a ritual New Year greeting and a hug for you all."[3]

The romantic, playful side of Guevara was also evident in his other writings and in his many speeches. That quality, combined with his good looks, personal charisma, and personal bravery in battling for what he believed was right, made him an appealing figure to many people both during his lifetime and after his death. Even some of Guevara's critics came to admire him because of the many fine qualities he possessed.

A Hispanic Hero

Today, Guevara is still revered by people in many countries as a symbol of resistance to governments that mistreat people. This is especially true in Latin America because he was born in Argentina. Additionally, historian Andrew Sinclair has written that Latin Americans have a special reverence for Guevara because he dared to challenge the United States, which had long dominated many of their region's countries politically and economically.

In his biography of one of the twentieth century's most notable revolutionaries, Sinclair wrote that Guevara gave millions of Latin Americans new hope for a better future. Sinclair claims Guevara did this by making them believe they could free their own countries from domination by their powerful neighbor to the north or, at the very least, initiate governmental reforms that could make life better for people living in their countries. Writes Sinclair: "History will probably treat Guevara as the most admired and loved revolutionary of his time [and] his influence, particularly in Latin America, must be lasting."[4]

Chapter 1

Growing Up in Argentina

Che Guevara was born on June 14, 1928, in Rosario, Argentina. He was christened Ernesto Guevara de la Serna, following the Hispanic tradition in which children also take on their mother's maiden name to honor them.

Guevara did not receive his most famous nickname, Che, until many years later. However, he acquired many other nicknames as a youth. His parents, Ernesto Guevara Lynch and Celia de la Serna y Llosa, lovingly referred to him as "Ernestito" or "Tete" when he was very young. When Guevara was in elementary school, fellow students named him "El Loco" (the crazy one) because of the playful pranks he loved to play, such as drinking ink out of a bottle or eating chalk. As a teenager, Guevara became known as "Fuser" because he played rugby so violently; it was a contraction of "El Furibundo [the furious] Serna," which he often shouted as he blocked or tackled opponents. In high school, he became "Pelado" (the shaved one) because he kept his hair very short. Guevara also earned one uncomplimentary nickname that referred to his lack of cleanliness: "They called me the Hog (*chancho* in Spanish) because I was filthy."[5]

Most of his nicknames reflect the fun he had with his friends; however, the most important experiences of Guevara's youth involved members of his family. Those events helped shape his attitude toward revolution.

A Revolutionary Family

Guevara's family was wealthy and belonged to Argentina's upper class. When Guevara was born, his father owned a plantation that grew maté, a bitter green tea that is popular in Latin

Che Guevara visits with his father, Ernesto Guevara Lynch, and his mother, Celia de la Serna y Llosa.

America. In later years, the elder Guevara engaged in other business ventures such as owning a company that built ships and buying and selling real estate. His mother came from a wealthy family that owned several ranches, and she had inherited a lot of money from her parents.

The Guevaras lived in luxury in large homes in Rosario and several other cities while Ernesto was growing up. His mother had servants who helped her care for Ernesto, the oldest of five children; he had two brothers and two sisters. Ernesto Sr. and Celia taught their children the importance of helping other people who were less fortunate than they were. Ernesto's parents and other members of his family were also willing at times to challenge traditional ways of doing things. Ana Lynch, Ernesto's paternal grandmother, campaigned for women's rights in the early twentieth century. During that time in Argentina, women were supposed to be content to live a life in which they were subordinate to men.

Ernesto's parents opposed Juan Perón, the dictator who ruled Argentina for several decades after he and other military officers seized power by force in 1943. "Celia and I were among Perón's active opponents," said the elder Guevara. "Celia was even arrest-

His First Asthma Attack

Che Guevara had to battle asthma for nearly his entire life. His father, Ernesto Guevara Lynch, describes his son's first asthma attack, which he suffered when he was just a few weeks shy of his second birthday:

On May 2, 1930—I remember the date so well—Celia and I set out with Tete [Ernesto] for a dip in the swimming pool. Celia was a strong swimmer and loved the water. The day turned out to be chilly and a brisk, cold wind blew. Suddenly Tete began to cough and wheeze. We took him straight to a doctor, who determined that the child had asthma. Perhaps he had caught a cold, or it could be that he inherited the disease, for Celia as a child had also been afflicted with it.

Quoted in I. Lavretsky, *Ernesto Che Guevara*. Moscow, Russia: Moscow Progress, 1976. www.chehasta.narod.ru/1stpart.html.

ed when, during a demonstration in Cordoba, she began to shout out anti-government slogans."[6] The Guevaras and other Argentinians had many reasons to dislike Perón. He had allowed poor housing, hunger, and illiteracy to flourish and then added to his nation's woes by levying heavy taxes on the citizens. He also allowed corrupt government officials to do as they wished. Many stole funds that could have been used for building schools, hospitals, and other public facilities. Perón also used brutality to fight anyone who challenged him politically. He created fear by imprisoning, torturing, and exiling his political foes.

The political activism of his parents and other relatives had a great effect on young Ernesto, who adopted their political and social ideas and values. There was another factor that helped shape the development of Ernesto's character while he was growing up—asthma, an illness that would trouble him his entire life.

Coping with Asthma

Ernesto had his first asthma attack on May 2, 1930, just a few weeks before his second birthday. His first bout with this disease lasted several days. He struggled so hard to breathe that his sister Ana Maria said years later that their parents "thought he would die."[7] Asthma is a medical condition in which people have trouble breathing because their lungs become congested. Asthma is triggered by allergies to air pollution, animals, chemicals, certain types of food, and plants. His mother had allergies and suffered from asthma, as did his siblings, but none of them was ever as ill as Ernesto, who had allergic reactions to many things, including fish and eggs.

When the bouts of asthma kept recurring, his parents started giving him injections of adrenaline to ease his labored breathing. Ernesto had to have so many shots for asthma attacks while he was a baby that "injection" was one of the first words he spoke. Even with injections, he often gasped for air when his asthma flared up. His lungs made a loud, rasping, wheezing noise as he painfully tried to breathe. During a severe asthma attack, people can suck air into their lungs, but congestion in their lungs makes it difficult for the oxygen to be transferred to their bloodstream. That is why some asthmatics seem to be choking to death during an attack.

Celia said her husband was so worried about their son during such attacks that he spent many nights holding the boy upright for hours to help him breathe: "[He] became accustomed to sleeping seated on the bed of his oldest son, so that the latter, reclining on his chest, could better bear the asthma."[8] While helping his son, Guevara himself often could not get any sleep.

When Ernesto was four years old, the Guevaras moved from Buenos Aires to Alta Gracia, hoping to take advantage of the drier climate and less polluted air. Although Ernesto's health improved a little, he did not go to school regularly until he was nine years old. His mother was his teacher for the first few years of his education. She taught Ernesto how to read and write, and she continued to tutor her son after he started attending school to make up for the many days he missed due to illness.

A Teacher Remembers Che

"He was an outstanding student. He looked and acted much older than he was, and was clearly already grown up with a definite personality, moody and undisciplined, but extremely mature."

John Gerassi, ed., *Venceremos! The Speeches and Writings of Ernesto Che Guevara.* New York: Macmillan, 1968, p. 6.

Like many young people confined to bed for long periods due to poor health, Ernesto became a voracious reader. He once told his friend Alberto Granado, "Every time I have an asthma attack or I have to stay indoors [I] spend two or three hours taking the opportunity to read what I can."[9] His father had a huge library, and the young Ernesto could choose from about three thousand books. Among his favorites were novels of adventure by authors like Miguel de Cervantes, Jules Verne, and Jack London. Ernesto also devoured social commentary by Latin American writers such as Ciro Alegría of Peru, Jorge Icaza of Ecuador, and José Eustasio Rivera of Colombia. The latter books were written for adults, and after reading them, Ernesto would talk to his father so he could better understand the ideas he had encountered.

Guevara rode this motorized bicycle 2,680 miles through Argentina in 1950.

Ernesto also loved reading poetry, especially verse by Pablo Neruda, a Chilean poet who later won the 1971 Nobel Prize for Literature. "He knew many poems by heart and had tried his own hand at writing verse,"[10] said his father. Despite his asthma and love of reading, Ernesto's youth was not sedentary. In fact, as he grew older, he became a good athlete.

Overcoming His Asthma

Doctors today tell people with asthma to exercise so they can strengthen their lungs and cardiovascular system, but in the

1930s, physicians thought strenuous activity would make asthmatics even sicker. Ernesto's father, however, believed exercise could help his son become healthier, so he pushed him to swim, hunt, and play sports like rugby, soccer, tennis, and golf. Although Ernesto's health improved as his body grew stronger from physical activity, he still had frequent asthma attacks. Because exercise can trigger asthma, this often happened while he was playing sports. When his breathing would become labored, Ernesto would head to the sidelines and give himself an injection. He would push the needle right through his shirt, inject the adrenaline, and then roar back into action.

The majestic twin waterfalls at Iguazu Falls National Park in northern Argentina inspired Guevara during his travels through his country.

Ernesto participated in sports with a passion that bordered on ferocity. In rugby, he tackled opponents harder than almost anyone else and was never afraid to challenge bigger players. Fernando Berrall, a childhood friend, admired Ernesto's courage, whether it was in playing sports or doing something else: "He was decisive, audacious, and self-assured, and above all, he was fearless. I remember that as being one of the most genuine of his character traits."[11] Ernesto displayed this reckless courage in rock fights with other neighborhood youths and daredevil stunts such as jumping from great heights into rivers or walking narrow pipelines suspended over deep ravines.

Even though his asthma attacks were sometimes so bad that his friends had to carry him home, Ernesto never quit trying to do everything they did. Roberto Guevara said he believes his brother's personality was shaped in part by his constant battle to overcome his illness: "He was a very sick boy, but his character and willpower allowed him to overcome it. Any task, no matter how daunting, could be solved by dint of enthusiasm, revolutionary fervor and unbending determination."[12]

High School Rebel

Guevara's teen years were unconventional in many ways. In 1941, the Guevara family moved to Córdoba, the capital of the province that had the same name. A year later, Ernesto Guevara enrolled in a public high school called Colegio Nacional Dean Fumes. Most children from wealthy families attended private schools, but the Guevaras wanted their son to be educated with children from many backgrounds.

The summer before he began high school, Guevara went on the first of several trips in Latin America. He told his parents, "I want to see things. I am going on a tour of Argentina, but I will be back in three months, in time for school."[13] Even though Guevara was only thirteen, his parents let him go. The youth attached a small motor to his bicycle and set off with only a small sum of money. While traveling through northern Argentina, Guevara often slept under trees because he could not afford a room. He also worked picking crops to earn money for food.

In high school, Guevara continued his unconventional lifestyle. He often got into trouble by clowning around and disregarding rules. He had begun smoking herbal cigarettes, which were supposed to help people with asthma, and he sometimes lit one during class despite rules against smoking. He left school whenever he wanted to do something else. His developing views of politics also got him into trouble. In class one day, he caused a stir when he claimed, "The military don't let the masses be educated, because if the people were educated, they would not accept their rule."[14] He was briefly expelled from school for criticizing the military; Perón and the military ruled Argentina with an iron hand. It was one of many disciplinary actions he earned through his rebellious behavior.

Although Guevara was willing to challenge authority even as a teenager, he believed it was senseless to do so unless one was well prepared. In 1943, his friend Alberto Granado was jailed for participating in a student protest against Argentina's military rulers. When Ernesto visited him, Granado told him he should organize more protests. The sixteen-year-old boy's response surprised his friend: "Take to the streets so that the police can beat us with clubs? Nothing doing. I will go out only if you give me a gun."[15] Even as a teenage boy, Ernesto realized it was dangerous to challenge Perón, who would not hesitate to have armed police or soldiers beat or kill protesters. He did not want to risk losing his life unless he had a chance to fight back.

What Che's Father Taught Him

"I taught Ernesto never to care about who his friends' parents were. Butcher and baker, they all came to our house, rich and poor, they were all welcome."

Ernesto Guevara Lynch, quoted in Martin Ebon, *Che: The Making of a Legend.* New York: Universe, 1969, p. 12.

Despite being a rebel and class clown, Ernesto Guevara was a good student. When he graduated from high school in 1947, his grades were good enough to allow him to enter the University of Buenos Aires.

Medical School

His father and many other people had believed Guevara would study engineering. Instead, he chose medicine. Historians believe his decision was influenced by his grandmother's death from a stroke, his mother's bout with breast cancer, and his own lifelong struggle with asthma. Whatever factors led him to choose medicine over engineering, Guevara decided to become a researcher. He hoped to find new ways to help people suffering from illness. Many years later, Guevara explained his career choice: "When I started out to be a doctor, when I began to study medicine, most of the ideas I now have as a revolutionary were absent from the storehouse of my ideals. I wanted to succeed, like everybody. I dreamed of being a famous researcher."[16]

By the time Guevara began attending the university in Buenos Aires, his parents had moved there. However, they were no longer wealthy. His parents had spent money lavishly for years, and his father's varied business interests had faltered. The downturn in family fortunes had begun while Guevara was in high school, forcing him to work for spending money as a night watchman, newspaper reporter, and a student employee at the Institute for Allergy Research.

To save money while attending medical school, Guevara lived at home. During summer vacations, he worked at several jobs, including male nurse on freighters that delivered cargo to Argentine ports. He also came up with several ideas for new businesses, including altering an insecticide designed for locusts so it could kill cockroaches. Although his business ventures failed, medical school proved easy for Guevara. He completed his first five years of coursework in just three years. Nothing held him back, not even his asthma. Beatriz Guevara, his favorite aunt, said, "We would listen to him gasping, studying lying on the floor to ease his breathing, but he never complained. For him it was a challenge."[17]

After completing his third year in medical school, Guevara set out on another long trip through Argentina. He departed Buenos Aires on January 1, 1950, again on a bicycle powered by a small engine. During the trip, the twenty-two-year-old Guevara for the first time began keeping a diary. Writing down

An Animal Lover

Che Guevara could be a ruthless revolutionary; he had no qualms about killing those who opposed him. But he also had a gentle side, one that he showed in his love for animals. In a collection of Guevara's writings, John Gerassi describes this kinder part of Guevara's personality:

> Another facet of Che's personality was his tendency toward senti-mentality. When the family dog died of old age, for example, [the thirteen-year-old Guevara] wept like any middle-class American kid. Then he called his gang [of friends] together and organized a funeral procession, carrying a handmade coffin through the streets of the town to an empty lot, and with a voice broken by sobs, delivered a heartrending eulogy before giving his friends the signal to lower the casket into the earth. Che's love for animals did not decrease as he grew older. In his last year of medical school, for example, despite protests from neighbors, he risked his life shinnying up a perilous pipe to rescue a sparrow who had caught his wing between two tiles on the roof.

John Gerassi, ed., *Venceremos! The Speeches and Writings of Ernesto Che Guevara.* New York: Macmillan, 1968, p. 3.

Che Guevara's love for children and animals is commemorated by this statue.

what happened each day as well as his reflections on his experiences became a lifelong habit. In six weeks, Guevara traveled over 2,680 miles (4,000 km) through a dozen provinces of Argentina.

On the trip, Guevara encountered a side of Argentina he had not seen before. He visited popular tourist spots. He traveled to poor areas in remote parts of the country where people lived on the edge of starvation and had little opportunity for a decent life. It was in such poverty-stricken areas that Guevara felt he truly came to know his homeland. One entry in the diary, which his father published after Guevara's death, describes his newfound understanding of his country: "No, one doesn't come to know a country or find an interpretation of life in this way [staying at rich resorts]. This is a luxurious facade, while [a country's true] soul is reflected in the sick of the hospitals, the detainees in the police station or the anxious passersby one gets to know."[18]

The Wanderer

Guevara returned to Buenos Aires in time for his fourth year of medical school. During that fourth year, Guevara experienced his first serious romance. He and Maria del Carmen Ferreyra became engaged to be married. They split up, however, before Guevara finished his medical studies. Ferreyra explained once why she believes this happened: "I think he saw me as a person who was going to be a burden to his life. As if I were an obstacle to the life he wanted, the adventurer's life. He wanted to travel, explore the world, look around."[19]

Even as a young man, Guevara knew that he would not be content to remain in Argentina. He wanted to travel and experience many things, and it was not long before he would get his wish.

Chapter 2

Ernesto Guevara Becomes the Revolutionary Che

After returning to school following his trip through northern Argentina, Guevara studied hard and once again progressed rapidly through the course of study to become a doctor. But he was torn by his continuing desire to travel and learn about the world outside his native Argentina. Ernesto Guevara Sr. once tried to explain his son's wanderlust. The older Guevara said: "There was something in his nature which drew him to distant wanderings, dangerous adventures and new ideas."[20]

In January 1952, Guevara surrendered again to that urge to travel when he and Alberto Granado decided to tour Latin America on an old, beat-up motorcycle. The ten-month journey took Guevara across South America, ending with a short flight to Miami, Florida. This trip, more than any other, marked a turning point in his life.

A Journey on La Poderosa

On January 4, 1952, the two friends climbed aboard Granado's 1939 Norton 500 cubic centimeter motorcycle and rode out of Buenos Aires. They were headed to a leper colony in Venezuela,

In a scene from the 2004 movie, The Motorcycle Diaries, *Che Guevara (front) and Alberto Granado journey through South America.*

where Granado was to begin working as a doctor. Guevara humorously nicknamed the motorcycle "La Poderosa," which in English means "the powerful one." The old motorcycle was anything but powerful. It kept breaking down, forcing them to stop repeatedly and make repairs for flat tires, engine problems, and even a broken frame.

The two adventurers also kept crashing the cycle; the record was nine times in one day. This happened because the roads they traveled were primitive, often nothing more than dirt and sand, and the bike was hard to balance due to clothing, equipment, and food they had strapped to its frame. Guevara kept a journal that was later published as *The Motorcycle Diaries: Notes on a Latin American Journey*. In it, he describes one bad fall early in the trip: "I took over the controls, accelerating to make up for precious lost time. A fine sand covered part of a bend and—boom: the worst crash of the whole trip. Alberto emerged unscathed but my foot was trapped and scorched by the cylinder, leaving a disagreeable memento which lasted a long time because the wound wouldn't heal."[21]

To reach Venezuela they rode north along South America's Pacific coast, through Chile, Peru, Ecuador, and Colombia. Because they had little money, they usually slept outside unless someone offered them shelter for the night. They had to work throughout the journey to buy food and other necessities, including medicine for Guevara's frequent asthma attacks. "We worked at odd jobs to earn a few pesos," said Granado. "We worked as stevedores, porters, sailors [and] we were capable of peeling potatoes and doing other odd chores, one of us with a university degree and the other nearly a graduate doctor."[22] They also earned money as soccer coaches and male nurses at a leper colony on the Amazon River.

While riding through Chile in February, their motorcycle broke down after yet another crash. "It was our last day as 'motorized bums,'" wrote Guevara. "The next stage seemed set to be more difficult, as 'bums without wheels.'"[23] Unable to fix the cycle, they had to continue their journey by walking, hitchhiking, rafting down the Amazon River, and even stowing away on a small ship by hiding in a filthy bathroom. When the stowaways were discovered, the ship's captain forced them to work to pay for their passage. One of their jobs was to clean their foul hiding place.

Sights That Changed Guevara

Guevara's diary vividly describes the beautiful scenery he and Granado saw and the enjoyable times they had, including playing soccer and romancing young women in various towns along the way. However, the most powerful parts of the book describe the poverty and social injustices that Guevara witnessed in various countries.

Accustomed to an affluent lifestyle, he was appalled at the squalid living conditions of many Latin Americans. In many areas, people lived in run-down shacks that lacked running water and indoor bathrooms and had only dirt floors. Guevara became aware of these conditions because people sometimes allowed him and Granado to sleep in their homes when they had no place else to stay. He was also troubled by the lack of health care. In Valparaiso, Chile, Guevara met an elderly woman who suffered from asthma. Because she was too poor to afford medical treatment, he gave her some of his own medicine. Guevara also became concerned that Latin Americans, who were mostly of Spanish descent, discriminated against native Indians, whom they considered inferior.

What made Guevara angriest of all was the way business owners treated their workers. In Machu Picchu, Peru, he discovered that business owners gave their workers coca for energy and so they could work longer hours. In its natural state, coca, the plant from which cocaine is derived, is a stimulant. Guevara knew that if the workers earned enough money to buy decent food, they would have had enough energy to do the work required.

Two Future Doctors

"[Che] Guevara and I remarked that this was pretty much what our futures would have been—me a small town pharmacist, he a doctor treating the allergies of wealthy ladies—if it weren't for that certain something that made us rebel."

Alberto Granado, after he and Guevara visited a friend who was a doctor in Argentina during their motorcycle journey. Alberto Granado, *Traveling with Che Guevara: The Making of a Revolutionary.* New York: Newmarket, 2004, p. 37.

Guevara was also distressed by what he saw at a copper mine in Chuquicamata, Chile. Guevara and Granado briefly worked there as guards. They felt the owners grossly underpaid the workers and failed to provide decent working conditions. "The company's grandeur is built on the ten thousand bodies lying in the grave-yard,"[24] he wrote. Because most of the large mines, agricultural concerns, and other big businesses in Latin America were owned or controlled by U.S. companies, Guevara blamed the United States for the way the workers were treated. But he also believed Chile shared responsibility for the abuses because it allowed the firms to operate the way they did: "The biggest effort Chile should make is to shake its uncomfortable Yankee friend from its back, a task that for the moment at least is Herculean, given the quantity of dollars the United States has invested and the ease with which it flexes its economic muscle."[25]

His view of the United States became even more negative when he reached Miami, Florida, in 1953. After the two travelers had reached Venezuela in July, they had split up. Granado began his new job at a leper colony. Guevara hitched a ride on an Argentinian airplane that was transporting race horses to Miami and stayed with friends there for a month. Guevara hated his time in Miami and later claimed that "those were the hardest and most bitter days of my life."[26] With little money, Guevara could do nothing but spend hours walking the streets of Miami. He grew to hate the United States even more because of the racism he witnessed against blacks—mainly the segregation that barred them from using the same restaurants and other public facilities that whites did. Guevara was also deeply troubled by the suffering he had seen in Latin America. He finally went home in late August after someone loaned him money for an airplane ticket.

"I Am Not the Same Person"

Guevara returned to school because he had promised his mother he would get his medical degree. He graduated in July 1953 as a doctor with a specialty in allergies. His motorcycle trip had transformed him, however, and medicine no longer interested him. In the preface to his diary, which he wrote after returning to Argentina, Guevara states, "The person who wrote these notes passed away the moment his feet touched Argentine soil again. The person who reorganizes and refines them, me, is no longer, at least I am not the same person I once was."[27]

Guevara had wanted to become a doctor to help people, but his journey made him believe he needed to do more for them than conduct medical research. He felt he should try to change the governments that ruled Latin American countries so they would be more responsive to the needs of average people.

Signs like this one were common in Miami and elsewhere in the South in 1953 when Guevara reached the United States for the first time.

Guevara believed that those countries should be more committed to improving the lives of their citizens by providing them with decent housing, more education, better health care, and greater economic opportunity. In a 1960 speech, Guevara explained his new attitude:

> Because of the conditions in which I traveled I came into close contact with poverty, hunger, and disease. I discovered that I was unable to cure sick children through lack of means, and I saw the degradation of undernourishment and constant repression. In this way, I began to realize that there was another thing which was as important as being a famous researcher [and] that was to help those people.[28]

On the trip, Guevara had come to believe that governments in Latin American countries had to become more committed to helping common people. He wanted to help make that happen.

On July 8, 1953, Guevara set out by train on a journey to see more of the world. In the back of his mind, however, he also wanted to find a situation in which he could do something to

Treating Lepers as Human Beings

During their journey through Latin America, Che Guevara and Alberto Granado visited a leper colony in Lima, Peru. In a letter to his father, Guevara described shaking hands with the patients. He hoped this would show them that the visitors accepted them as human beings. Guevara wrote:

> Their appreciation sprang from the fact that we never wore overalls or gloves, that we shook their hands as we would anybody's,

that we sat with them, talking about all sorts of things, that we played football [soccer] with them. It may all seem like pointless bravado, but the psychological lift it gives to these poor people—treating them as normal human beings instead of animals, as they are used to—is incalculable and the risk to us [of catching leprosy] is extremely low.

Ernesto "Che" Guevara, *The Motorcycle Diaries: Notes on a Latin American Journey.* New York: Ocean, 2004,

In this scene from The Motorcycle Diaries, *Che Guevara and Alberto Granado leave a leper colony in Peru on a homemade raft.*

help make life better for his fellow Latin Americans. As he bid good-bye to his parents, he shouted out, "Here goes a soldier for [Latin] America!"[29]

Revolution in Guatemala

After brief stops in several countries, Guevara headed to Guatemala. Guevara went there because President Jacobo Arbenz was creating the type of social changes he believed Latin America needed. Elected in 1951, Arbenz had given more citizens the right to vote so that wealthy property owners could no longer control Guatemala as they had in the past. He had also begun seizing agricultural land that the United Fruit Company was not using and giving it to the poor to live on and farm. United Fruit was a giant U.S. firm that controlled much of Latin America's agricultural production.

When Guevara arrived in Guatemala City in December 1953, he stayed at the home of a friend. Unable to find work as a doctor, mainly because he was from another country, he first sold encyclopedias and later got a low-paying job in a medical laboratory in Guatemala's Department of Sanitation. Even though Guevara was barely making enough money to rent a room in a cheap boardinghouse, in January he wrote to his family about his admiration for Guatemala: "This is a country where you can breathe deep and fill your lungs with democracy."[30] It was also a place where he could meet many interesting people like Hilda Gadea, who was a member of Peru's liberal Aprista Youth Movement. Gadea, who a year later would marry Guevara, said they were drawn together by common political ideas: "In our countries the struggle was [to] reach true social justice, a fight against [economic] exploitation, hunger, ill health, illiteracy, and the dismal levels of life in our villages. These were the immediate tasks that must absorb our energies."[31]

Gadea worked in Guatemala's Department of Economic Studies. She and Guevara both backed the political changes Arbenz was making in Guatemala. Some Guatemalans, however, feared that Arbenz was going to make their country a Communist nation because he was backed by the Communist Party, which was strong in Guatemala. One of those who opposed communism was Carlos Castillo Armas, a former Guatemalan army officer who had fled to Honduras in 1951 after a failed military coup. In June 1954, Castillo Armas, tried again. He led a small army into Guatemala, seizing control of the country. Castillo Armas succeeded this time because he had help from the U.S. Central Intelligence Agency (CIA), which wanted to keep communism out of Latin America. Castillo Armas was unable to retain control of Guatemala, however, and for the next three decades the country was fractured by civil war.

Members of Guatemala's small army joined with civilian Arbenz supporters in an effort to repel the Castillo Armas attack. One of the civilians who took part was Guevara. He tried to organize young men to fight. "It was necessary to resist and

Guatemalan president Jacobo Arbenz, who was much admired by Guevara, addresses his countrymen.

almost no one wanted to do it,"[32] he later lamented. When the new regime tried to arrest Guevara because he had opposed the invasion, he sought sanctuary at the Argentine embassy. Guevara was trapped in the embassy for two months, until Argentinian officials arranged political asylum for him in Mexico.

Guevara arrived in Mexico City on September 21, 1954. His plan was to spend about six months there and then satisfy his longing to see the world by touring the United States, Europe, and even China. His stop in Mexico City, however, would change his plans.

A New Life in Mexico City

During the train trip to Mexico City, Guevara acquired a new friend—Roberto Cáceres, a Guatemalan who was fleeing because he had also backed Arbenz. The two rented a small apartment and, with an old camera, began making a living by taking photographs of tourists.

Ernesto Guevara Evades the Argentine Draft

In his final year of medical studies at the University of Buenos Aires, Che Guevara had to report for a physical that would determine if he would be inducted into the army. Guevara opposed Argentine dictator Juan Perón, so he used a trick to make sure he failed the physical:

He showered in freezing water before being examined by the medical commission, triggering an asthma attack, thanks to which he was declared unfit for military service. As his mother would say years later: "If Commandante Che Guevara had had to spend a year doing the shopping for a first lieutenant's wife or polishing the cartridge belt that his superior would never use it would have been a shameful absurdity. But he was declared unfit. There was justice after all."

Quoted in Jorge G. Castañeda, *Compañero: The Life and Death of Che Guevara.* New York: Knopf, 1997, p. 55.

Many of the people Guevara took pictures of were U.S. citizens. Even though they were his customers, Guevara did not like them, because he believed U.S. businesses were exploiting Latin American workers to make huge profits. One day when a U.S. tourist told him to go away, Guevara's anger at Americans boiled over: "You may laugh now, but our day will come."[33] Although Guevara was eventually hired in 1955 as a physician at General Hospital of Mexico, where he did some research in allergies, his pay was so low that he began working as a news photographer for the Latina News Agency.

In his spare time, Guevara studied political theory. He hoped to find new ways in which Latin American countries could more fairly govern their people. Guevara became a convert to communism after reading books by Karl Marx, the nineteenth-century German philosopher who created the political and economic theories underlying communism, and Vladimir Lenin, the first Russian Communist leader. Under this political system, the government controls businesses and other sectors of the economy. This is done so that profits can be shared by all citizens, not just business owners and rich people (who Communists called capitalists). In a letter to his mother, Guevara stated: "I believe they [Communists] are worthy of respect and that sooner or later I will join the Party."[34]

Gadea had also fled to Mexico City, and when the two met again, they fell in love. When they married on August 18, 1955, their best man was Raúl Castro. Gadea had introduced Guevara to Castro that June, and the two men had quickly become friends. In July, Raúl Castro arranged for Guevara to meet his brother Fidel. The meeting would change Guevara's future as well as the history of Cuba.

Guevara Meets Fidel Castro

Raúl Castro had come to Mexico City to find a home for his brother, who had been released from prison in Cuba in May 1955. Fidel Castro had been jailed after trying to overthrow Cuban dictator Fulgencio Batista in July 1953. Castro tried to oust Batista because Batista was a corrupt leader who ignored the needs of Cubans. Batista was a military officer who had seized power and ruled the island brutally. Many government officials under him were corrupt, stealing funds intended to educate and provide social services to the population. In Mexico City, Castro immediately began plotting a return to Cuba for another attempt at ousting Batista.

Guevara and Castro met at a dinner party hosted by a supporter of the Cuban revolutionary. Guevara was fascinated by Castro and sat spellbound for hours as he explained his plan to invade and seize control of Cuba. When Castro discussed his reasons for wanting to overthrow Batista, Guevara realized Castro had the same goal he did: to give Cubans more opportunities for a better life. That first night they met, Guevara became a convert to Castro's cause and volunteered to help him: "I talked with Fidel throughout the night. By morning I was already enlisted as a doctor in the forthcoming expedition [invasion]. As a matter of fact what I experienced during my wandering through Latin America ending with the event in Guatemala, it wouldn't have taken much to convince me to take part in a revolution against any tyrant."[35]

Castro was happy to have a doctor who could treat his soldiers when they were wounded or sick. But he also valued Guevara for his political philosophy, which he admitted years later was more advanced than his own thinking: "Ideologically speaking and [from] a theoretical point of view he had a better background, he was more advanced as a revolutionary."[36]

Che Meets Fidel Castro

"An Argentine by birth, he was Latin American in his spirit, in his heart. It was a matter of minutes for Che to join that small group of us Cubans who were working on organizing a new phase of the struggle in our country."

Fidel Castro, quoted in Tad Szulc, *Fidel: A Critical Portrait*. New York: William Morrow, 1986, p. 326.

Guevara's willingness to join an armed revolution did not surprise Gadea, who claimed that the CIA-sponsored takeover in Guatemala had taught Guevara a valuable lesson: "It was Guatemala which finally convinced him of the necessity for armed struggle and for taking the initiative against imperialism. By the time he left, he was sure of this."[37]

Fidel Castro (left) and Che Guevara share a quiet moment as friends and comrades in 1956.

Becoming Che

When Guevara met Castro, he took his final step toward becoming a revolutionary by committing himself to violently overthrowing the government of a country. It was also during the period in which he began associating with the Cuban rebels that he acquired the nickname "Che," which is an affectionate slang term in Argentina for "pal" or "buddy." Because Guevara used the word so much to refer to everyone else, the Cubans began to call him that. Castro once explained the nickname: "Che wasn't Che then. He was Ernesto Guevara. It was because of the Argentine custom of calling people 'che' that the Cubans began calling him Che. That was how he got that name, a name he later made famous, a name he turned into an emblem."[38]

Chapter 3

Che Helps Bring Revolution to Cuba

On February 15, 1956, Che Guevara and his wife, Hilda Gadea, had a daughter they named Hilda Beatriz. When Fidel Castro came to see the newborn infant at the couple's small apartment in Mexico City, he made a prediction: "This girl is going to be educated in Cuba."[39] It seemed a bold, almost foolish boast for a political exile who hoped one day to retake his country—if need be by force. But when Castro spoke those words, Guevara had already been working for months on invasion plans for Cuba. Guevara would help in more ways than one to make Castro's promise to his daughter come true.

Preparing for an Invasion

By December 1955, Guevara and other Castro followers began actively preparing for the invasion. The group called themselves the 26th of July Movement in honor of Castro's failed 1953 Cuban revolt. The conspirators first worked to improve their physical conditioning. To lose weight, Guevara quit eating bread, pasta, and the steak he usually had for breakfast. He and the Cubans rowed on a lake in Chapultepec Park, performed calisthenics, and practiced hand-to-hand combat techniques. At a ranch outside Mexico City near Chalco, they learned to use rifles and other weapons and performed military maneuvers like marching at night. In April 1956, Castro named Guevara leader of the Chalco training camp. It was an honor for Guevara, especially because he was the only non-Cuban.

Despite Castro's attempt to keep the conspiracy secret, Cuban intelligence officers discovered he was planning some type of

Guevara looks on as Castro salutes cheering Cubans on January 1, 1959, the day they entered Havana after overthrowing dictator Fulgencio Batista.

A Letter to His Wife

Che Guevara and Raul Castro (left) in Cuba's Sierra de Cristal Mountains in 1958.

On January 28, 1956, Che Guevara wrote a letter to his wife, Hilda, to explain what had happened to him in his first two months in Cuba. He told her:

I am writing you these burning Martian [José Martí a nineteenth-century fighter for Cuban independence] lines from the Cuban [wilderness]. I am alive and thirsting for blood. You might say that I'm really a soldier (at least I'm dirty and in tatters), for a mess-kit is serving as my writing desk, a gun is slung over my shoulder and a new possession—a cigar—stuck between my teeth. Things haven't been easy. You already know that we ended up by fault of our navigator in some fetid undergrowth, and our misfortune continued until we were attacked in the already notorious Alegría de Pío and had to scatter like pigeons. I was wounded in the neck [and chest] and remain among the living only thanks to my [many] cat's lives for a bullet from a machine-gun found my cartridge case which was slung around my chest, and from there it ricocheted against my neck.

Quoted in Hilda Gadea, *Ernesto: A Memoir of Che Guevara.* Garden City, NY: Doubleday, 1972, p. 168.

action against Batista and alerted Mexican officials. On June 25, 1956, police arrested Castro, Guevara, and other conspirators for plotting to overthrow Batista. Although Castro was freed on July 24, Guevara was imprisoned until mid-August. Before Castro left the prison, he told Guevara, "I will not abandon you."[40] When Castro finally bribed officials to release the rest of his men, Guevara's loyalty to him deepened.

Guevara was the group's medical officer and held the rank of lieutenant. Although he returned to the invasion preparations with even greater zeal, Guevara admitted that getting ready was harder than ever because the conspirators feared being arrested again: "The days passed, we worked secretly, hid where we could, avoided public appearances as much as possible, and in fact almost never went out in the street."[41] Despite the added difficulty, Castro bought a battered 38-foot (11.6m) motorboat called the *Granma*—its American owner had nicknamed it after his grandmother—which he kept in the Mexican seaport city of Tuxpan.

On November 25, 1956, Castro, Guevara, and eighty-one other men departed Mexico for Cuba in the small, crowded boat. Although Castro's bid to overthrow Batista would succeed, the historic venture began with a string of mistakes and near disasters.

The Invasion's Rocky Beginning

The boat ran into a storm not long after hitting the open sea. Built to hold no more than twenty people, the overloaded vessel rocked so violently that almost everyone became seasick. Guevara could do nothing to relieve the symptoms, because he had forgotten to bring seasickness pills. The men were too sick to eat, which was perhaps a blessing, because the group had also failed to pack enough food for the voyage.

The *Granma* was scheduled to land at Niquero in Oriente Province on November 30. There, Castro and his men were to rendezvous with a group of supporters in an attempt to seize the city of Santiago. The Cubans were led by Frank País, a former student activist who backed Castro. But the overloaded ship made poor time, sailed off course, and finally ran aground on

December 2 far from their destination on a sandbar near Las Coloradas. In addition to arriving too late to help País, their landing site was a nightmarish swamp. As they struggled to wade ashore through mud and chest-high water, they lost almost all of their supplies. Guevara suffered an asthma attack and had a tough time getting to dry land.

The worst was yet to come because Batista had been alerted about the invasion by informers. After quelling the revolt in Santiago staged by País's group, Batista's soldiers began searching for Castro's men and soon discovered where they had landed. On December 5, while Castro's men were near Alegría de Pío eating sugarcane, the only food they had, Batista's men attacked. Many of the rebels were wounded or killed, and the rest fled in terror. Guevara was wounded. He describes what it felt like to be hit by a bullet: "I felt a terrible blow on the chest and another in the neck, and was sure I was dead [and] I immediately began to wonder what would be the best way to die. I remembered an old story of Jack London's in which the hero, knowing that he is condemned decided to end his life with dignity."[42]

In fact, Guevara had only suffered minor wounds to the neck and throat. After firing back at the enemy soldiers, he managed to escape. In the next sixteen days, Batista's men pursued Castro's men and killed or captured all but fifteen of them. Guevara, Fidel and Raúl Castro, and a dozen others finally managed to find safety in the Sierra Maestra, a rugged mountain range. In this isolated location, Castro reorganized his men into a fighting force and began planning his attack on Batista.

The Rebels Attack

The devastating defeat actually worked in Castro's favor. Believing that he had eliminated the rebels, Batista quit pursuing them. Castro then contacted his Cuban supporters, who helped him get weapons, food, and other supplies. New recruits also began joining his small force.

On January 22, 1957, Castro decided it was time to quit hiding and strike back at Batista. In a daring night raid on an army barracks near the La Plata River, the rebels defeated fifteen soldiers, killing two of them and wounding five while suffering no injuries themselves. The victorious rebels seized needed supplies from the well-stocked barracks and returned to their mountain refuge. Guevara said the small skirmish had a huge impact on Castro's attempt to win control of Cuba: "The effect of our victory was electrifying. It was like a clarion call, proving the Rebel Army really existed and was ready to fight."[43] The daring raid won new supporters for Castro's Cuban Revolution by establishing him as a realistic threat to Batista.

The attack set a pattern for the military operations of Castro's tiny band of revolutionaries. Because Batista's army of fifty thousand dwarfed the rebel force and had nearly unlimited supplies from

Key aides (including Guevara, second from left) surround Fidel Castro in June 1957 in a secret jungle base near the Cuban coast.

the United States, the rebels resorted to guerrilla tactics. Guerrilla warfare is a specialized form of warfare that pits small groups of men against larger numbers of soldiers who are better armed and trained. Guevara, once rejected by the Argentine military because of his asthma, became a master of this unconventional type of combat.

Che's Guerrilla Strategy

In the first few months of 1957, Guevara's main duties were to care for sick and wounded rebels. But Guevara also took part in combat and quickly gained an understanding of the tactics. Guevara fearlessly conducted raids and other military actions against Batista's army and was wounded several times. On December 9, 1957, in the Battle of Altos de Conrado, he was shot in the foot. Because Guevara had become so astute at directing guerrilla operations, Castro warned him after that battle to be more careful, because he was too valuable a fighter to lose. Castro angrily told him, "I order you not to take on any combat role. Take charge of directing people well, which is the indispensable task at this time."[44] Despite Castro's advice, Guevara continued to engage in combat while directing other soldiers in battle.

Che Looked Ordinary

"I had imagined him to be a tall, stocky man [but] he made no special impression on me when I did see him; in fact, I was rather disappointed. He was a skinny, ordinary guy like any of us, and I exclaimed 'So this is Che?'"

Alberto Castellanos, quoted in Paco Ignacio Taibo II, *Guevara, Also Known as Che.* New York: St. Martin's, 1997, p. 136.

Oniria Gutiérrez, who joined the rebels when she was only seventeen, remembers one battle in which airplanes were bombing and shooting at the group Guevara commanded. She explains what she saw after she and others sought shelter: "I was behind some rocks and when I lifted my head up, I saw Che standing there, calmly smoking his pipe and observing how the

Che Chooses Bullets, Not Medicine

Because Che Guevara had never experienced combat, it was believed that his most important contribution to the effort to win control of Cuba would be as a doctor. However, on December 5, 1956, just three days after the rebels landed in Cuba, he became an armed combatant. When Cuban soldiers attacked the rebels while they were resting in a cane field, Guevara had to decide whether to carry away medicine or bullets. He explains what he did:

> At that moment a comrade dropped a cartridge [bullet] box at my feet. I pointed question-ingly to it and the man answered with "It's too late for bullets," and he immediately left. This was perhaps the first time I was faced with the dilemma of choosing between my dedication to medicine and my duty as a revolutionary soldier. At my feet were a pack full of medicines and a cartridge box; together, they were too heavy to carry. I chose the cartridge box, leaving behind the medicine pack, and crossed the clearing which separated me from the cane field.

Che Guevara, *Reminiscences of the Cuban Revolutionary War*. New York: Grove, 1968, p. 44.

planes swooped down."[45] Impressed by his bravery, Gutiérrez went and stood by his side.

It was Guevara's military leadership, however, and not his bravery in combat that was most important to helping Castro fight Batista. In 1963, Guevara published *Guerrilla Warfare*, a classic text that is still studied by military leaders. In a 2001 article in *Military Review*, Captain Steve Lewis commented favorably on the tactics Guevara formulated: "Although not considered a strategic military genius, Guevara's effective, realistic principles served him well. They included mobility, movement by night, careful use of ammunition [supplies], flexibility, careful study of the ground [on which the fight occurs] and surprise and fury [in staging attacks]."[46]

The Battle of Uvero marked Guevara's emergence as a valued guerrilla commander. Up until then, the rebels had usually attacked at night; they could move freely then because their opponents tended to stay indoors after dark. But on May 28, 1957, the rebels raided a small military installation during the day to catch the enemy by surprise. Although the rebels for once outnumbered the soldiers eighty to fifty-three, it was difficult to attack a defended position. But Guevara boldly led his men in the attack despite the danger—one soldier next to him was shot to death. Afterward, Guevara was promoted to commandante (major), the highest rank in Castro's army.

Though pleased by the promotion, Guevara believed the real significance of the battle was that it marked a turning point in Castro's effort to overthrow Batista: "From this battle on, our morale grew tremendously, our decisiveness and our hope for triumph increased also [because] we were already in possession of the secret of victory."[47] Before leaving Uvero, the rebels seized a huge quantity of weapons and other supplies. Guevara gathered medicines, some for his asthma but also some for treating the many poor Cubans they would meet along the way.

Wooing the Cubans

Guevara preferred the excitement of combat to doctoring civilians, but he understood the importance of winning new backers for Castro's cause. Rural Cubans, or campesinos, suffered from a variety of illnesses such as premature aging, malnutrition, parasitic infections, and rickets. Guevara realized many of these ailments resulted from poverty, poor diet, and bad working conditions—all tolerated under (or even created by) Batista's regime. Seeing this, the rebels became even more determined to overthrow Batista: "We began to feel in our flesh and blood the need for a definitive change in the life of the people."[48]

By the second half of 1958, Castro's forces controlled most of Oriente Province. They began providing medical care to residents and set up schools for children and adults, many of whom were illiterate. The rebels also established a radio station and newspaper and built seven landing strips for airplanes. Most importantly, Castro initiated land reform. He took land owned by wealthy

Cubans and U.S. firms like the United Fruit Company and gave small parcels to campesinos to live on and farm. He also halted the high rents that campesinos had to pay to wealthy landowners for such land. These moves won thousands of new supporters for Castro. Guevara claimed, "We were advancing with the Land Reform as a spearhead of the rebel army."[49]

Batista imprisoned, tortured, and executed people who opposed him, including wounded soldiers captured after battle. By contrast, Castro's men treated civilians and enemy soldiers humanely in an effort to win their support. Guevara believed doing such things was

Che Guevara commands the rebel force that captured Santa Clara, Cuba, on December 30, 1958.

an important part of waging a successful guerrilla war: "Conduct toward the civilian population ought to be regulated by a large respect for all the rules and traditions of the people in order to demonstrate effectively, with deeds, the moral superiority of the guerrilla fighter over the oppressing soldier."[50]

While Castro was battling Batista's forces in rural areas in 1957 and 1958, his supporters were also fighting back in the cities. They staged protests and work strikes to weaken support for Batista's regime, bombed military targets, assassinated Batista officials and supporters, and attacked military installations.

Defeating Batista

Gradually, more and more Cubans began to side with Castro, because they believed he offered them a chance for a better life. Realizing the balance of power was shifting to the rebels, Batista in May 1958 launched a powerful offensive against Castro and his men in the Sierra Maestra area. Castro's men, however, withstood the superior force of ten thousand soldiers, and Guevara claimed the offensive's failure "broke the back of the Batista

Cuban children wave a flag with the likeness of Che Guevara in a 2004 celebration of Batista's overthrow and Castro's victorious arrival in Havana.

army."[51] The army's failure to defeat Castro demoralized soldiers, and many deserted. Some of the soldiers even joined the rebels they had been sent to fight. In August, Castro decided it was time to leave the safety of the Sierra Maestra for a final push to defeat Batista. He split his forces into three units. The column Castro led would take control of the rest of Oriente Province and capture the city of Santiago. Raúl Castro headed a group that was to attack and harass Cuban soldiers in the eastern part of the island. Guevara was ordered to take 180 men and capture Las Villas Province in central Cuba. Guevara guided his men to victory as they defeated Batista's forces in cities such as Sancti Spíritus, overwhelmed army installations, and cut railroad lines to make it harder for Batista to send new forces against them.

Guevara's most important battle took place on December 30, 1958, in Santa Clara, the province's capital. His men defeated a much larger force and even captured an armored troop train trying to flee. The city of 150,000 was a railroad and communications center and housed Leoncio Vidal Barracks, the largest military facility in central Cuba. On January 1, Guevara sent aides to negotiate the surrender of soldiers who had barricaded themselves in the barracks. The message they sent back surprised him. Said Guevara: "The news was astonishing . . . Batista had just fled [Cuba], causing the collapse of the [Cuban army]."[52]

That was how Guevara learned that the war was over. Realizing that he could no longer withstand the rebels after the loss of Santa Clara, Batista that morning had fled Cuba. Castro had finally succeeded in ousting Batista and taking control of Cuba.

Not Satisfied with Victory

Guevara was happy and exhausted after forcing Batista to leave. But when a joyous rebel claimed they had won the revolution and asked Guevara for time off to visit his family, Guevara denied his request. Guevara told him, "No, we've won the war. The revolution begins now."[53] Guevara realized that the military victory had been only the first and easiest step in the Cuban Revolution. Now came the much more difficult battle of transforming the social and political lives of Cubans.

Chapter 4

Che: A Man of Many Titles

Che Guevara arrived in Cuba's capital city of Havana on January 2, 1959, just a few days after his victory at Santa Clara. Guevara enjoyed the jubilant cheers that greeted him and the other rebels. He was even happier a week later when he had a joyous reunion with family members who flew to Cuba.

Guevara's parents had hoped he would return to Argentina after having helped Castro win power, but he told them he would remain in Cuba. His father, who wanted his son to work as a doctor, was especially disappointed. Guevara told him: "I know I left medicine behind some time ago. Now I'm a fighter working to prop up a government."[54] In the next few years, Guevara performed many different tasks for Castro. The doctor-turned-military-leader would serve as a political adviser, urging Castro to adopt the Communist model for Cuba. Guevara would also play the role of economist, directing Cuba's financial rebirth, and roving diplomat, forging political and economic alliances with other nations.

His first post was announced on January 2 when Castro appointed Guevara military commander of La Cabaña, an army fortress overlooking Havana's harbor. In this new role, he had the responsibility for overseeing efforts to restore order to Havana following the fall of Batista's regime.

Che the Executioner?

Havana was in turmoil because of the uncertainty over Castro's government, continuing clashes with members of Batista's defeated army, and looting. Guevara's men ended the violence and brought order to Havana. Guevara was also given the task of arresting and trying soldiers and former government officials who were accused of various crimes, such as the imprisonment,

Contentment shows on Guevara's face in a photograph taken a few days after his victory at Santa Clara.

torture, and murder of thousands of Batista opponents. Officers in Batista's army, for example, had ordered soldiers to kill captured rebels after battles. About five hundred soldiers and former government officials were found guilty and executed for such crimes.

The fact that Guevara had been given such a job surprised many people; it seemed a minor position for so high-ranking a member of Castro's army. Historians believe Castro chose Guevara for that job because he knew Guevara would not hesitate to execute people who had committed crimes against Cubans. During the revolution, Guevara had shown a willingness to kill anyone who betrayed the rebels. After Guevara ordered one such death, he explained to a friend who was horrified by his action, "Look, in this thing either you kill first or else you get killed."[55] Guevara himself had shot Eutimio Guerra in 1956 after the former rebel tried to lead Cuban soldiers into the Sierra Maestra to attack Castro's men.

In overseeing the trials and executions, Guevara developed a reputation as a cold, ruthless killer. Some said he pronounced many suspects guilty even if the evidence seemed less than overwhelming. But Manuel Piñeiro, a rebel who became a high-ranking official under Castro, defended Guevara: "He was not an ogre capable of assassinating people with little or no justification. He was very demanding with the lawyers and prosecutors who were applying revolutionary justice against the [suspects] who had been responsible for torturing and murdering combatants and women."[56]

A Knowledgeable Economist

"Guevara knows and understands finance and economics, and he knows exactly where he is going [with his plans for the Cuban economy]. It was just like talking to another banker, except he is an orthodox Marxist."

U.S. Treasury Department official Walter Sauer after meeting with Che Guevara in 1959, quoted in John Gerassi, ed., *Venceremos! The Speeches and Writings of Ernesto Che Guevara.* New York: Macmillan, 1968, p. 15.

Guevara believed the trials and executions were necessary. He said the need to give the Cuban people justice for the crimes that had been committed justified them and that he was only carrying out the people's will. Said Guevara: "The executions by firing squads are not only a necessity for the people of Cuba, but also an imposition by the people."[57]

There is some doubt, however, about how much direct control Guevara had over the trials. When exhaustion and asthma made him deathly ill, he left Havana on January 17 to recuperate at a seaside home in nearby Tarara. Although he was able to do paperwork and conduct meetings with people, Guevara was bedridden for much of the next few months.

During the period in which Guevara commanded La Cabaña, he also opened a school to teach illiterate soldiers to read and write. At the same time, Guevara was also helping to educate Castro about the virtues of communism and why this political and economic system would benefit Cuba.

Che the Communist

On February 7, 1959, the Cuban government granted Guevara citizenship for having helped oust Batista. In a television address on February 12, he thanked the Cuban people for the rare honor and promised to work to improve their lives. He said the most important way to do that was to continue the land reform that had begun during the revolution. Said Guevara: "Today we are set on going to the big landholdings, even on attacking and destroying them. The rebel army is ready to carry [land] reform through to its final consequences."[58] Guevara felt it was wrong that two thousand wealthy individuals and foreign companies owned nearly half of Cuba's land. He believed the government should control the land so that any earnings from farming and industry could be channeled into public services.

Guevara's comments were more radical than any by Castro. They made officials in other nations believe Cuba was turning into a Communist nation because his proposal to have the state control land was a main tenet of communism. Castro, however, had not yet decided whether communism would work in Cuba. During a trip to the United States in April 1959, he said, "I am not a Communist, nor do I agree with Communism," and a month later in Havana stated that "capitalism can kill a man with hunger. Communism can kill him by destroying his liberty."[59]

Che Refuses Special Treatment

Che Guevara never tried to use his fame or powerful government position to make money. Elias Entralgo, an official with the University of Havana, once offered to pay Guevara to give a lecture at the school. In response, on August 31, 1964, Guevara wrote Entralgo that he would not give the lecture because the offer of a speaking fee had angered him:

> I have received your kind invitation, which demonstrates to me—without your intending it, I am sure—the radical differences of opinion that separate us on the question of what is a leader. [It] is inconceivable that a monetary remuneration be offered to a leader of the government and the party for any kind of work. As far as I personally am concerned, the most treasured of all payments which I have received is the right to belong to the Cuban people [the citizenship which had been granted him], a right which has no equivalent in pesos [dollars] or centavos [pennies].

Che Guevara, *Reminiscences of the Cuban Revolutionary War*. New York: Grove, 1968, p. 281.

In the next year, as Castro tried to figure out how to govern Cuba, he relied heavily on Guevara for advice. And Guevara, a committed Communist since he had studied political theory in Mexico, convinced Castro that communism would enable the Cuban leader to enact the radical economic and social changes he believed were necessary to make life better for Cubans. One of Guevara's main arguments was that the government needed to own Cuba's means of production. These included land, factories, and other businesses that produced goods Cubans bought and sold to other countries. Guevara argued that the government needed to own and control the means of production so that it could distribute the profits throughout Cuba. That theory was the heart of Communist philosophy.

Guevara biographer Andrew Sinclair states flatly that "it was Che who actually converted [Castro] to Communism as a doctrine."[60] Although Castro did not publicly declare Cuba to be Communist until December 1, 1961, Guevara had adopted Communist principles before that to transform Cuba's economy.

Transforming Cuba's Economy

On October 7, 1959, Guevara was named director of the National Institute of Agrarian Reform. On November 25, he was named president of the National Bank of Cuba. On February 21, 1961, he became minister of industries. Together, these roles placed him squarely in charge of Cuba's economy. No one was more surprised than Guevara at his new role as the country's economic leader: "If anyone had told me when we embarked on the *Granma* (I was the unit's doctor), that I would be one of the country's economic organizers, I would have laughed at the thought."[61] Guevara, who once tended to sick people, now had to try to heal the shattered Cuban economy.

A construction crew working on a housing project near Havana gets help from Guevara (center) in 1962.

With his customary zeal for hard work, Guevara sometimes worked thirty-six hours straight in his new jobs. He studied economic and financial theory and consulted with experts to acquire a thorough knowledge of the subject. He visited agricultural and industrial sites throughout Cuba and conferred with visiting economic officials from other countries. Foreign dignitaries were surprised and sometimes shocked upon meeting Cuba's chief economic official. Like Castro and other rebels, Guevara continued to wear his trademark beret and to dress in olive military fatigues instead of business suits. And like his fellow *barbudos* (Spanish for "bearded ones"), he still had the beard that rebels had worn while battling Batista.

Guevara began revamping the island's economy by seizing privately owned land and creating huge state-owned farms on which poor rural Cubans lived and worked. The Cuban government also took over, or nationalized, telephone and electric companies, mines, factories, hotels, gambling casinos, and other businesses. Much of the land and many of the companies were owned by foreigners; U.S. businessmen alone claimed Cuba seized more than $3 billion in private property from them. Guevara also established new industries and attempted to diversify Cuba's agriculture, which depended almost solely on sugar.

His goal was to create an economy that would benefit all Cubans and not just wealthy individuals or big companies. Guevara once described what he was trying to accomplish in a letter to a friend: "The society of wolves [capitalists] is being replaced by another variety, not possessing the desperate impulse to rob his fellow man."[62]

Guevara's efforts made life better for many Cubans by providing more people with jobs and social services such as education and medical care. But he failed to strengthen Cuba's overall economy, partly due to circumstances beyond his control but sometimes because of his own mistakes.

Struggling with the Economy

The biggest problem Guevara faced was Cuba's economic dependence on sugar; three-fourths of the money Cuba earned from other countries came from the sale of sugar. Before Castro

Divorce and Remarriage

Friends surround Che Guevara and Aleida March on their wedding day.

Che Guevara was reunited in Havana, Cuba on January 1, 1959, with his wife, Hilda Gadea, and their daughter, Hilda, after not having seen them for more than two years. Guevara spoiled the happy occasion by announcing that he wanted to marry another woman. Gadea agreed to divorce him because he was so important to the Cuban Revolution. Gadea explains:

> With the candor that always characterized him, Ernesto forthrightly told me that he [wanted to marry Aleida March]. The pain was deep in me, but, following our convictions, we agreed on a divorce. I am still affected by the memory of the moment when, realizing my hurt, he said, "Better I had died in combat." Though I was losing so much at that time, I [realized] he had to have remained alive. He had to build a new society. No, I was happy that he had not died in combat, sincerely happy, and I tried to explain it to him. [Guevara responded,] "If that's how it is, then it's all right . . . friends, and comrades?" "Yes," I said.

Quoted in Hilda Gadea, *Ernesto: A Memoir of Che Guevara.* Garden City, NY: Doubleday, 1972, p. 171.

came to power, the United States had been Cuba's main trading partner, buying nearly all the sugar it produced. But in July 1960, U.S. president Dwight Eisenhower barred further purchases because he believed Cuba was turning Communist. His decision created an economic crisis by cutting off Cuba's main source of income.

The economic boycott was part of the Cold War, the political and economic conflict between capitalist and Communist nations that began at the end of World War II and continued through the breakup of the Soviet Union in the late 1980s. The boycott was one way in which the United States, the most powerful capitalist country, could use its economic power to weaken Communist nations. The boycott gladdened Guevara, who hated the United States and believed it was bad to be so financially dependent on one nation. Cuba, however, soon found

A worker harvests sugar cane on a Cuban plantation.

itself bound even more tightly to yet another nation. Unable to find other buyers for its sugar, Cuba finally agreed to exchange its entire crop each year to the Soviet Union for economic aid and oil, tractors, and other products it could not manufacture.

Although Guevara would later admit that "without Russian aid we'd starve,"[63] he was angry that one country again held so much economic power over Cuba. To ease that dependence, Guevara started factories to make products Cubans needed, from shoes to shovels. But he failed to realize that the small island nation did not have the raw materials or technology to produce many of the needed items. As a result, many new industries he started failed.

Time Magazine Praises Che

"Wearing a smile of melancholy sweetness that many women find devastating, Che guides Cuba with icy calculation, vast competence, high intelligence and a perceptive sense of humor."

Quoted in Jorge G. Castañeda, *Compañero: The Life and Death of Che Guevara.* New York: Knopf, 1997, p. 179.

Another problem Guevara ran into was the poor quality of many things Cuba produced. When the government had nationalized existing industries in Cuba, many technical experts and managers fled the country because they did not want to live under communism. Without them, Cuban workers did not have the expertise to make quality products. After visiting a soft drink plant, Guevara complained that "Coca-Cola, which we used to drink the most of, now tastes like cough medicine. [Why] can't we make a cola as good as or better than the Americans?"[64] The failure was especially galling because the popular beverage was considered a worldwide symbol of the success of U.S. capitalism.

Guevara tried to motivate Cubans to work harder, which he believed would strengthen the economy, but his efforts largely failed. In speeches and articles, he compared workers to rebel fighters and said they had a duty to work hard to make products their fellow Cubans needed. Putting it dramatically in combat terms, he once said, "The worker who, in moments of danger, deserts his trench, that is to say his machine, is failing in his fundamental duty."[65] The problem with this approach was that it tried to motivate workers by appealing to their sense of duty to other Cubans instead of offering them what they wanted, which was higher pay so they could have a better standard of living.

Guevara's mistakes were compounded by other factors that weakened the Cuban economy. For example, in the 1960s, bad weather led to reduced sugar crops several years in a row. In an October 18, 1965, report, the CIA claimed that by late 1963, "Guevara's policies had brought the economy to its lowest point since Castro came to power."[66] Despite the economic problems, Guevara remained popular. One way Guevara did that was to work side by side with average Cubans at tasks like cutting cane in sugar fields or even digging ditches. And unlike some leaders, Guevara was willing to admit his decisions had not always been right. "I made mistakes, and some of those mistakes are being paid for dearly,"[67] he once said.

As Cuba's top economic official, Guevara traveled all over the world to promote his country and make business deals. And because Guevara was the best-known rebel after Castro, he also undertook high-profile diplomatic tasks such as speaking at the United Nations and meeting with leaders of other countries. But his zeal to spread revolution wherever he went often made his attempts at diplomacy as unsuccessful as his efforts to revive the shattered Cuban economy.

Diplomat and Worldwide Traveler

His first diplomatic journey began on June 13, 1959, when he left Cuba on a three-month global tour that took him to a dozen countries, including Egypt, Japan, India, Indonesia, Pakistan, and Yugoslavia. Although Guevara switched from fatigues to dress suits for the trip, he often struggled with formal social settings and diplomatic ceremonies, and in India he admitted that "new and complex protocols make me panic just like a child."[68] Although Guevara could be charming, he often made remarks that were undiplomatic. When he met Gamal Abdel Nasser, he angered the Egyptian president by telling him Egypt's reform efforts had not been radical enough because Nasser had not evicted Europeans who had previously owned large plantations.

The August 8, 1960 edition of Time *magazine featured a story about Guevara and his skill in managing the Cuban economy.*

In the fall of 1960, Guevara visited Communist countries in Europe as well as China to seek trade agreements after the United States began its economic boycott. He also represented Cuba at various economic summits, including one for Latin American countries in Uruguay in August 1961. To ease fears many people had that Cuba wanted to promote revolution in other countries, Guevara promised that Cuba would not "export revolution" by sending arms to rebels who were even then seeking to overthrow some Latin American governments. But he added, "What we cannot ensure is that the idea of Cuba will not take root in some other country."[69]

Guevara's inability to refrain from praising the Cuban Revolution or stating that a certain country needed a similar revolt often created discord. In a December 11, 1964, speech to the United Nations General Assembly in New York, he claimed that Cuba was a shining example to other nations "that peoples can liberate themselves" from domination by capitalist countries like the United States. Three days later, on the *Meet the Press* television show, Guevara said that revolutions like the one in Cuba are caused by the way people are treated: "Revolutions are not exported: they arise from the conditions of exploitation that the governments of Latin America inflict on their people."[70] Guevara was so effective in arguing for revolution that some Latin American governments contacted U.S. officials to complain that he should not have been allowed to appear on the show.

A New Site for Revolution

Following his New York visit, Guevara embarked on a three-month diplomatic tour of Asia, Europe, and Africa. In a speech in Algiers, Algeria, on February 24, 1965, to the Organization of Afro-Asian Solidarity, he again encouraged poor countries to fight back against rich, powerful countries that he claimed tried to control them economically and politically. Said Guevara: "There are no frontiers in this struggle to the death. We cannot remain indifferent in the face of what occurs in any part of the world. A victory for any country against imperialism is our victory, just as any country's defeat is our defeat."[71]

The speech was his last major appearance on the international stage. After Guevara returned to Cuba on March 14, 1965, he disappeared from public view for several months. When Guevara finally emerged from isolation, he was back in Africa. This time he was trying to lead an armed revolution like the one he had helped stage in Cuba.

Chapter 5

Failure in Africa

Shortly after entering Havana in January 1959, Guevara had described the elements that he believed brought success in Cuba. "We have demonstrated that a small group of men who are determined, supported by the people and without fear of dying can overcome a regular army. [However,] we must first make agrarian revolutions, fight in the fields, in the mountains, and from there take the revolution to the cities."[72]

In March 1965, Guevara set out to repeat once again that success. This time, he focused his efforts on the African nation of the Congo, which is known today as the Democratic Republic of the Congo.

Why Che Left Cuba

Although many people were surprised Guevara chose Africa, those who knew him well had always known that he intended to leave Cuba one day to lead a revolution somewhere else. In 1961, when Guevara was named to oversee the Cuban economy, he had told his secretary, Manuel Manresa, that he and Manresa would not stay in Cuba very long: "We'll stick this out for five years and then we'll be off. We can still fight a guerrilla war when we're five years older."[73] He had also warned Castro that he would only remain a short time because he wanted to continue to spread revolution. Although Guevara left Cuba willingly, the timing of his departure was triggered by two other factors—his increasing disenchantment and tense relationship with the Soviet Union and the potential for revolution in the Congo.

Guevara had been thwarted in trying to reshape Cuba's economy by the Soviet Union, which dominated Cuba economically and politically. Guevara wanted the Soviets to help Cuba increase its industrial capacity to make it less dependent on buying products from other countries. Instead, the Soviets forced Cuba to continue to concentrate on producing sugar,

Che Guevara wears his trademark beret in this 1965 photograph, taken the same year he went to the Congo in Africa.

which they needed for countries they controlled. Guevara also believed that the Soviets forced Cuba to accept trade agreements that made Cubans pay too much for many products, which he believed was a form of economic theft similar to capitalism.

His most stinging criticism of the Soviets came in his February 24, 1965, speech to the Organization of Afro-Asian Solidarity in Algiers. Guevara said Communist nations should always work to help each other. But he added that when one nation took advantage of another economically, "we must agree that [such] nations are, in a way, accomplices of imperialist exploitation."[74] Guevara did not name the Soviets, but everyone knew which country he meant.

Guevara also denounced the Soviet Union for being too timid in opposing the United States. He was especially angry about the Cuban Missile Crisis in October 1962, when Soviet premier Nikita Khrushchev backed down in a tense confrontation with U.S. president John Kennedy and agreed to remove nuclear missiles from Cuba. Guevara had helped persuade the Soviets to give Cuba the missiles, which he believed Cuba needed to make the United States afraid to attack it. Guevara criticized the Soviets for allowing Cuba to lose a powerful defensive weapon. Said Guevara: "If the rockets had remained, we would have used them all and directed them against the very heart of the United States, including New York, in our fight against [capitalist] aggression."[75]

The final factor that led Guevara to leave at that particular time was what he had learned during his 1965 African trip. In Algiers, Guevara had told a journalist that prospects for a successful revolution were good in several countries: "Africa represents one of the most important, if not the most important, fields of battle against all the forms of [economic and political] exploitation existing in the world [and] there are big possibilities for success in Africa."[76] Guevara believed the best chance for success was in the Congo. He believed he could help Congolese rebels take control of their country by passing on guerilla warfare strategies. He believed he could help them create a new society by teaching them Communist ideology.

Castro met Guevara when he returned to Havana on March 14, 1965. In a long talk that night, Guevara told Castro he wanted to go to the Congo to help Communists win control of that nation. Castro immediately began working to help Guevara fulfill his dream of taking revolution to another country.

Che Leaves for Africa

In what marked his last official appearance in Cuba, Guevara on March 22 spoke about his African tour to members of the Ministry of Industries, the agency he headed. He finished by saying he was going to Oriente Province for a month to help harvest sugarcane. It was a believable lie because he had worked in the sugar fields in past. His real destination was the Congo, and he left for that country on April 2, 1965.

Guevara had always been a highly visible Cuban official. As the weeks passed without any public appearances or news about his activities, people began to wonder what had happened to him. When Castro and other officials refused to comment on where he was, rumors started about his possible fate. The most popular theory, one that was reported in newspapers around the world, was that Castro had killed Guevara because he either feared Guevara was hurting relations with the Soviets or because he was jealous of Guevara's growing fame. Other reports claimed Guevara had gone to help North Vietnam fight South Vietnam and the United States in the Vietnam War or that he was somewhere in Latin America stirring up revolution.

Castro did not want to tell the truth about Guevara because he feared that U.S. intelligence officials and other anti-Communists would try to find him and kill him. Castro finally stated on April 20 that Guevara was alive and someplace where he would be of "most use to the revolution."[77] His statement was purposely vague to protect Guevara. He did not comment on Guevara in detail until October 3, when he read a letter from Guevara during a televised ceremony of the Communist Party of Cuba.

In the letter, which Guevara had given to him on March 31, Guevara explained that he was leaving Cuba because "other nations of the world call for my modest efforts." Although Guevara did not name his destination or explain what he was doing, he claimed his new task was "the most sacred of duties: to fight against imperialism wherever it might be." Guevara also formally resigned his government positions and party titles and gave up his Cuban citizenship, which he had once valued so highly. He explained that although it pained him to leave "a people who received me as a son," he wanted to sever his ties to Cuba so that country would not be held accountable for his actions: "Nothing legal binds me to Cuba. [I] free Cuba from any responsibility."[78]

Guevara severed his ties so that anti-Communist countries would not retaliate against Cuba for what he did. His move also protected Cuba from the wrath of the Soviet Union, which opposed direct military involvement by Cubans in other countries. The Soviets feared such activity might lead the United States to act against Cuba. If that happened, the Soviets would have to defend their Communist ally, and it could lead to a global war. Castro admitted years later that making Guevara's letter public had been a political necessity.

The letter failed to clear up where Guevara had gone. In fact, Guevara's involvement in the attempted revolution in the Congo would be shrouded in secrecy for many years.

Che Says Good-bye to His Parents

Che Guevara sent a farewell letter to his family in Argentina before he left for Africa in 1965. In saying good-bye, he once again likened himself to the fictional character Don Quixote. Guevara throughout his life closely identified himself with the kind-hearted adventurer.

Once again I feel beneath my heels the ribs of Rocinante [Quixote's horse]. Once more, I hit the road with my shield upon my arm. [In 1956 before leaving for Cuba,] I wrote you another letter of farewell. As I remember, I lamented not being a better soldier and a better doctor. The latter no longer interests me. I am not such a bad soldier. . . . Now, a will power which I have polished with delight will sustain some shaky legs and some weary lungs. I will do it. Give a thought once in a while to this little soldier of the twentieth century. For you, a hug from your obstinate and prodigal son.

Ernesto Guevara, *Che Guevara Speaks: Selected Speeches and Writings*. New York: Merit, 1967, p. 142.

Che Goes to the Congo

Guevara was unrecognizable when he departed Cuba. He had shaved his head and wore a dental prosthesis to disguise his features so that he could travel secretly. On April 19, Guevara and 130 Cuban soldiers arrived in Dar es Salaam in Tanzania, a country that borders the Congo. All the soldiers were labeled "volunteers" to protect Cuba from their involvement in the attempted revolution, but Castro had ordered some of them to accompany Guevara.

Some of the soldiers had fought with Guevara in Cuba, and nearly all of them were of African descent. Guevara believed that would help them be accepted by the rebels who were trying to overthrow President Moise Tshombe. The Congo had received its independence in 1960 from Belgium, which had ruled it as a colony since 1885, but warring factions had battled over it since then.

Tshombe had finally won control of the Congo with the support of the United States and South Africa, which was ruled by racist whites. Many Congolese and Africans in neighboring countries opposed Tshombe because he maintained ties with Belgium and ruled brutally with the help of white mercenary soldiers. Like the Congo, Tanzania and several other African nations in the 1960s had won their freedom from European nations that had ruled them as colonies. Those nations believed so deeply that blacks had to rule African nations without the help of whites that they had invited Guevara to help two pro-Communist groups overthrow Tshombe. The groups were led by Pierre Mulele and Laurent-Désiré Kabila.

Che Never Wanted to Stay in Cuba

"Comrade Guevara joined us during our exile in Mexico, and always, from the very first day, he clearly expressed the idea that when the struggle was completed in Cuba, he would have other duties to fulfill in another place."

Fidel Castro, quoted in Leo Sauvage, *Che Guevara: The Failure of a Revolutionary.* Englewood Cliffs, NJ: Prentice Hall, 1973, p. 32.

On April 23, Guevara and the Cubans traveled by boat across Lake Tanganyika, on the border of Tanzania and the Congo, and

Guevara enjoys a few moments with a villager's baby and a local rebel while in the Congo.

set up a base camp for their operations in a Kibamba village. Because Guevara did not want anyone to know he was in Africa, he assumed the code name "Tatu," the Swahili word for the number three. For the next seven months, the man known as Tatu would try to help the rebels win control of the Congo. The period would be the most frustrating and humiliating of his entire life.

Failure in the Congo

As was his habit, Guevara kept a diary. The one he wrote in the Congo, which was published after his death as *Reminiscences from the Revolutionary War (The Congo)*, opens with the following summation of his experience there before he departed in

Guevara, shown in one of the few photos of him without a beard, leaves the Congo in 1965.

November: "This is the history of a failure [and] in my view, any importance the story might have lies in the fact that it allows the experiences to be extracted for the use of other revolutionary movements."[79] There were two main reasons Guevara failed in his revolutionary mission—his faulty understanding of the political and social situation in the Congo, and of the methods of the Congolese rebels.

Guevara knew that the key to defeating Batista had been that a majority of Cubans had united against the dictator. In the Congo, the various factions were not united. And to Guevara's dismay, the rebels he was dealing with were not trying to win the support of their fellow Congolese. Instead of treating people well to turn them into allies, the Congolese rebels, who were known as the People's Liberation Army, bullied them. This contrasted starkly with Guevara, who tried to win them over by treating their illnesses as he had done in the Sierra Maestra. At the end of May, Guevara showed his disgust for the rebels in his journal: "The main feature of the People's Liberation Army is that it was a parasite army which didn't work, didn't train, didn't fight, and demanded supplies and labor from the [local] population, sometimes by force. It is clear that an army of this sort can be justified only if it occasionally fights [but] it didn't even do that."[80]

Guevara claimed Congolese rebels were lazy, drank heavily, and did not follow orders during training: "The human element failed. There is no will to fight [by soldiers, and] the leaders are corrupt."[81] Guevara was also upset that rebel leaders were hesitant to fight. But when Guevara finally prodded them into attacking the Bendera garrison on June 29, it was a military disaster. The raid failed because many rebel soldiers fled in terror when the first shots were fired.

Four Cubans died in the battle. One of the slain Cubans was carrying a diary that fell into the hands of the CIA. The CIA was trying to keep Tshombe in power so his country would not become Communist. The diary made it clear that Cubans were helping the rebels. The CIA began to suspect that Guevara, who had disappeared so mysteriously from Cuba, was leading the Cubans. It took several months, but the CIA finally confirmed that Guevara was in the Congo when captured rebels identified him from pictures.

President Moises Tshombe was an unpopular leader in the Congo, causing Guevara to conclude the country would support revolution.

Although the rebels had some successes, Guevara became increasingly disenchanted with their lack of discipline. In a letter to Castro in October, he complained, "There are plenty of armed men, but we lack soldiers. [We Cubans] can't liberate by ourselves a country that does not want to fight."[82] Guevara's mood was also blackened by his health. He was ill during his entire stay in Africa from a fever that he and many of his men contracted, from asthma, and from a two-month bout with diarrhea. Daniel Alarcon Ramirez, one of the Cuban soldiers, claimed Guevara began to lose the ability to think clearly and make competent decisions. Said Ramirez: "His state of mind was not even at half capacity. He was fading day by day and was always in a bad mood. [We] realized this was not the Che we knew. We asked ourselves, 'What's wrong with Che?' One of us went to ask him and was scolded for his trouble."[83]

A Revolutionary in Exile

As the Congo situation deteriorated, Castro began to believe Guevara could not win, and on November 4 he wrote a letter urging him to leave. Guevara refused to quit but was soon forced to depart because of political changes.

Che Was a Popular Doctor

"A legend developed in short order. Wherever we went, we found we were known because of Dr. Tatu [Che Guevara's code name], a white medic. Although we had other medics, people came to Dr. Tatu to be treated."

Harry Villegas, quoted in Paco Ignacio Taibo II, *Guevara, Also Known as Che*. New York: St. Martin's, 1997, p. 431.

Tshombe was dismissed from office in October 1965 after a political struggle with other Congo leaders. President Joseph Kasavubu, who succeeded Tshombe, then tried to appease Tanzania and other neighboring countries that had invited Guevara to the Congo. Kasavubu promised to make changes such as getting rid of white South African mercenaries who had helped Tshombe stay in power. With this change, Guevara's help was no longer needed.

A Retreat That Was an "Inglorious Spectacle"

In November 1965, Che Guevara and about two hundred Cuban soldiers evacuated the Congo after they failed to ignite a Communist revolution. Guevara wrote that he was filled with despair while waiting for boats that would carry them across Lake Tanganyika to safety in Tanzania:

> Moreover, who was I now? [I] could not bring myself to demand the final sacrifice of remaining behind. I spent the final hours like this, alone and perplexed, until the boats eventually put in at two o'clock in the morning. Our withdrawal was a mere flight, or worse. It was a plaintive, inglorious spectacle; I had to chase away men who kept imploring us to take them too; there was no element of grandeur in this retreat, no gesture of defiance. The machine-guns were in position, and I kept the men at the ready, as usual, in case [opposition forces] tried to intimidate us by attacking from the land. But nothing like that happened. There was just a lot of grumbling, while the leader of the would-be escapees cursed in time with the beating of the loose moorings.

Ernesto Guevara, *The African Dream: The Diaries of the Revolutionary War in the Congo.* New York: Grove, 2000, p. 216.

Guevara left the Congo on November 21. He went to the Cuban embassy in Dar es Salaam, where he stayed seven weeks. Guevara needed to rest and recuperate because he was in bad shape physically—he weighed less than 110 pounds (50kg) after having lost 50 pounds (22.7kg) due to illness. He also began working to complete his Congo diary and started two more manuscripts, one on philosophy and the other on economics. In Dar es Salaam, Guevara was joined by his new wife, Aleida March. March and Guevara had married in June 1959 after Gadea and Guevara divorced. The two had met during the campaign to overthrow Batista. For once, Guevara was able to enjoy time with his family. Though he loved them, he had spent very little time with them over the years.

Father and sons share a rare moment together. Here, Guevara is pictured with Camilo and his infant son Ernesto.

When Guevara had departed Mexico to fight in Cuba, he left behind Hilda, his first child. By the time he ventured into the jungles of the Congo, he had had four more children with his second wife, including Ernesto, who was born February 24, 1965, a little more than a month before Guevara secretly departed Cuba. And while Guevara was in the Congo, his mother became sick and died. He had always loved her, and not being able to say good-bye hurt him deeply. Guevara had once commented on the sacrifices he and others had to make in pursuing their political goals: "Sometimes we revolutionaries are lonely. Even our children look on us as strangers. They see less of us than of the soldier on sentry duty, whom they call 'uncle.'"[84] For Guevara, the revolution took precedence over everything else— even family.

A Fateful Decision

The Congo debacle was the greatest failure of Guevara's life. He spent six months in seclusion, first in Africa and then in Europe pondering the future. Castro asked him repeatedly to return to Cuba, but Guevara refused because he wanted to try again to stage a revolution in another country. This time, however, he would make the attempt in Latin America, an area he understood much better than Africa.

Chapter 6

Failure and Death in Bolivia

Che Guevara entered Cuba in July 1966 on a fake passport that identified him as Ramón Benitez Fernández of Uruguay. Guevara did not want the CIA to know where he was. He feared that if the CIA learned he was in Cuba, it might try to interfere with his next attempt at revolution.

Guevara believed many countries were ripe for armed revolution because many governments were exploiting their citizens. He commented on this on April 16, 1967, in an impassioned statement to the Organization of Solidarity of the Peoples of Africa, Asia and Latin America, a pro-Communist group. He praised North Vietnam, which was then fighting South Vietnam and the United States in the Vietnam War, and said he believed there was a need "to create a second or a third Vietnam . . . many Vietnams" in other countries. Guevara said that that need was especially great in the part of the world he knew and loved the most: "In Latin America the armed struggle is going on in Guatemala, Colombia, Venezuela, and Bolivia; the first uprisings are cropping up in Brazil. Almost all the countries of this continent are ripe for a type of struggle that, in order to achieve victory, cannot be content with anything less than establishing a government of socialist tendencies."[85]

A much different image of Guevara appeared in the April 1967 issue of Tricontinental, *a magazine published in Cuba.*

Guevara's remarks became his most famous defense of armed revolution, but he did not deliver them in person. He had written them several months earlier, and they were transmitted to the Organization of Solidarity after officials in Cuba released them to the news media. They were released that way because Guevara was already in Bolivia stirring up revolution.

Planning for Bolivia

Guevara had high hopes for success in Bolivia. It already had a Communist movement. It also had a huge population of rural poor and a government run by René Barrientos, an air force general who had seized power in 1964 through a military coup. When Guevara explained his reasoning to Fidel Castro, the Cuban leader agreed to support the effort with weapons and other supplies.

For his new venture, Guevara contacted old friends and recruited about twenty volunteers. In August, Guevara began training the small force in a remote area of Cuba. In addition to weapons instruction and brutal physical conditioning that included long marches with heavy packs, he made them learn Quechua, the language of Bolivia's native Indian population.

Despite the physical and emotional scars he still bore from his Congo failure, Guevara was excited about Bolivia. Said Cuban official Manuel Piñeiro: "He was like a new kid with a toy—he was euphoric."[86]

Che Enters Bolivia

To avoid detection by foreign intelligence agents, Guevara disguised himself before leaving Havana on October 23, 1966. He plucked his hair to become nearly bald, wore thick glasses, and used a dental prosthesis to change the shape of his face. Guevara's attempt to keep his movements secret also included traveling under a false identity—Adolfo Mena Gonazález of Uruguay—and taking a circuitous route to Bolivia that included stops in Moscow, Russia, and São Paulo, Brazil.

Guevara reached La Paz, Bolivia, on November 3 and four days later arrived at a large farm that Bolivian Communists had purchased to serve as the base camp for his guerrilla campaign. The 3,700-acre (1,500ha) tract of land was located near the Ñancahuazú River in the central Andes Mountains. The site in

Guevara altered his appearance by changing his hairstyle and wearing glasses for the fake passport he used to enter Bolivia.

southeastern Bolivia was chosen for its remoteness from large cities and its proximity to the borders of adjoining Brazil, Argentina, and Paraguay. Guevara hoped one day to bring revolution to these and other Latin American countries. The base could house about one hundred men and included a large lecture room for training sessions, ovens to make bread, and communications systems.

Upon his arrival, Guevara supervised the excavation of caves to store food, weapons, medicine, and documents. He began growing back his hair and beard and wrote in his diary that "in a few months I shall look like myself again."[87] The effort to ignite a revolution in Bolivia, however, would not progress as swiftly as Guevara's return to his normal physical appearance.

Guevara was unable to accomplish much in the first two months because of a lack of new recruits. Mario Monje, head of the Bolivian Communist Party, did not send Guevara the men he had promised. When Monje finally came to the Ñancahuazú camp on December 31, he stunned Guevara by demanding that he, Monje, lead the revolt because only a Bolivian could succeed. Guevara refused. "I would be the military leader and would accept no ambiguities on this score,"[88] he wrote in his diary.

A Prediction of Failure

"When the people find out that this guerrilla movement is being led by a foreigner, they will turn their backs on it and refuse to support it. I am sure it will fail because it will be led by a foreigner instead of a Bolivian."

Mario Monje, quoted in Jorge G. Castañeda, *Compañero: The Life and Death of Che Guevara.* New York: Knopf, 1997, p. 356.

That prideful decision turned Monje against Guevara and denied him the help of the Bolivian Communists Monje led. It was the first of many missteps in Bolivia.

Mistakes in the Bolivian Jungle

Despite Monje's treachery, Guevara obtained recruits from Moises Guevara, a Communist union leader for Bolivian mine workers.

Becoming Better Through Hardship

On August 8, 1967, while laboring through the jungle to evade pursuing soldiers, Che Guevara was so frayed emotionally that he used his whip to slash open the neck of the horse he rode. It was a loss of control for which he apologized to his men later that night. In his diary, Guevara wrote:

> I gathered everyone together and spoke along the following lines: we are in a difficult situation. Pacho [Alberto Fernandez] is recuperating, but I am a real mess, and the episode with the mare proves that at times I have lost control. [We] have reached a moment when great decisions are called for. This type of struggle provides us the opportunity to become revolutionaries, the highest level of the human species. At the same time, it enables us to emerge fully as men. Those who are unable to achieve either of these two states should say so and abandon the struggle. [In] short we must be more revolutionary and exemplary in our conduct.

Ernesto Che Guevara, *The Bolivian Diary of Ernesto Che Guevara.* New York: Pathfinder, 1994, p. 250.

After training the small combined force of about fifty men in guerrilla tactics, Guevara began launching hit-and-run attacks on the Bolivian army similar to those he had orchestrated in Cuba. The first occurred on March 23, 1967, when Guevara's men ambushed a group of eighty Bolivian soldiers, killing seven, wounding four, and taking fourteen prisoners. Before releasing the captured soldiers, Guevara treated their wounds in a bid to win them and other Bolivians over to his side.

The twenty-thousand-man Bolivian army greatly outnumbered Guevara's small rebel force of about fifty men. The Bolivians also had far superior weapons, including helicopters, airplanes, and bombs. As in Cuba, when Guevara had outmaneuvered another larger, better-equipped army, his guerrillas successfully attacked soldiers in a series of raids and skirmishes. But even while Guevara was winning many small military victories in Bolivia's mountainous Camiri region, he was steadily losing the overall campaign to overthrow Barrientos.

In April, soldiers discovered the rebel camp on the Ñancahuazú farm, probably with the help of local peasants. The discovery robbed Guevara of his base of operations. Perhaps more importantly, it showed the lack of support of the local population. Guevara mentioned this in his diary when he wrote that "the peasant base is still not developing . . . we have not made a single recruit."[89] In the eleven months of his guerrilla campaign, not one peasant joined Guevara.

The failure to attract peasants was devastating because Guevara needed more fighters to overthrow Barrientos. Guevara even tried to woo them by treating their illnesses; the tactic had worked in Cuba but failed in Bolivia. The peasants refused to join Guevara because he and the men he led were foreigners. The rural population would only support another Bolivian. Monje had tried to tell Guevara that, but he had refused to take the advice. Guevara also underestimated the popularity of Barrientos, who had promised Bolivians land reform, increased education, and the right of workers to form unions.

Even though Guevara never had as many fighters as he wanted, he was so skilled at guerrilla warfare that the Bolivian army could not stop him. Thomas Hughes, a Latin America intelligence specialist with the U.S. State Department, claimed in a report that "the failure of the army to deal effectively with a handful of insurrectionists shook the entire Bolivian government."[90] Guevara's military success continued through August 1967. However, Guevara's good fortune ended when a beleaguered Barrientos asked the United States for help.

U.S. Involvement Dooms Guevara

The U.S. government, which wanted to avert more takeovers like the one in Cuba, was already supplying Barrientos with weapons and other supplies because he opposed communism. To meet the new threat, the United States sent to Bolivia some Green Berets, members of its elite army unit, and CIA agent Félix Rodriguez. Their mission was to coordinate the activities of the Second Ranger Battalion, a special unit the Bolivian army had formed to hunt down Guevara and his men. The expertise the U.S. forces had in guerrilla warfare, some of it gleaned from reading Guevara's book on such tactics, helped the combined force begin closing in on the rebels.

The first big success came in August 1967, when the Bolivian-American force located the caves where Guevara had stored supplies, documents, and photographs. Guevara was in some of the captured pictures, which confirmed his presence in Bolivia. After learning what had happened, Guevara began his August 14 diary entry by calling it "a black day" and claimed the seizure was "the hardest blow they have dealt us." The huge cache of supplies had included Guevara's personal medication, and he admitted, "Now I am condemned to suffer asthma indefinitely."[91] His diary includes many references about his asthma, which sometimes was so bad that he could not travel with his men.

Though the revolution was always foremost in this thoughts, Guevara took time to visit with a Bolivian farmer and his children.

Why Guevara Failed in Bolivia

Che Guevara believed he could ignite a revolution in Bolivia because the situation there was similar to that in Cuba in 1956. Gordon Ho McCormick, a military expert on guerrilla warfare and terrorism, says Guevara failed because key elements present in Cuba were missing—the widespread popular support of Bolivians and opposition to the government. McCormick explains:

> As [Guevara] had written some years before, "to try and carry out [a guerrilla war] without the support of the population is a prelude to inevitable disaster." Che's inherent optimism [led] him to grossly overestimate the ease with which he and his guerrilla band would be able to recruit a popular following. . . .

Barrientos was widely viewed as an authentic Bolivian nationalist and had received a mandate to continue his reform program in popular elections held the previous July, in which he received 62 percent of the vote. Again, Che appears to have overlooked his own advice. As he had written in 1960, "Where a government has come into power through some form of popular vote, fraudulent or not, and maintains at least an appearance of constitutional legality, the guerrilla outbreak cannot be promoted, since the possibilities of peaceful struggle have not yet been exhausted."

Gordon Ho McCormick, "The Legacy of a Revolutionary Man," *World Policy Journal*, Winter 1997/98, p. 79.

Guevara's small force continued to receive food, weapons, and other supplies from a small band of Communist supporters. This vital supply line was cut off on September 18 when government agents arrested fifteen of the supporters. Guevara encountered other problems, too. His radios kept breaking down, making contact with officials in Cuba and supporters in Bolivia a constant struggle. Communications with allies and getting supplies became even more difficult in Guevara's final months in Bolivia when his unit was virtually isolated from the rest of the world.

The forces pursuing Guevara had scored a significant military victory on August 31 when they killed or captured nine of his men. Soldiers caught up with Guevara's band again on September 26 in the village of La Higuera, and in the battle he lost three more men, which reduced the number under his command to sixteen. After narrowly eluding the pursuing soldiers, the guerrillas were able to relax for a few days in a wooded area. When their need for food made them move again, their risk of being sighted increased.

"I Am Che Guevara"

On October 7, while the rebels were encamped in the Churro Ravine near La Higuera, Guevara wrote, "Today marks eleven months since our guerrilla inauguration." In what would be his last diary entry, Guevara commented about an elderly woman his men had talked to that day. After failing to get any information from her about enemy soldiers, Guevara wrote, "They gave her [money] and asked her to keep quiet, but held out little hope she would do so, despite her promises."[92] The woman did remain silent, but a man who also saw them did not.

Guevara went to sleep the night of October 7, 1967, knowing that government soldiers were positioned all around him. What he did not know was that earlier that evening, a farmer named Pedro Peña had seen his men enter the ravine while he was watering his potato patch. At dawn on October 8, Peña walked two miles to La Higuera to report what he had seen to Bolivian officials. Peña's story seemed to confirm suspicions that Guevara was in the area.

Acting on the tip from the farmer, Captain Gary Prado led two platoons of Bolivian soldiers to the ravine. After positioning his men, Prado attacked the surrounded guerrillas at 1:30 P.M. During the battle, Guevara was shot in the right calf. Bleeding from his wound and suffering yet another asthma attack, Guevara tried to escape. He was helped by a Bolivian miner, Simon Cuba Sarabia, who had joined the rebels. But with the miner half-carrying Guevara, they ran into three soldiers. Guevara surrendered peacefully, saying, "I am Che Guevara and I have failed."[93]

The Death of Guevara

A gleeful Prado radioed news of the capture of the famed guerrilla to his superiors. He then ordered four soldiers to use a blanket as a litter to carry the wounded Guevara to La Higuera. After getting there about 7:30 P.M., Prado placed Guevara in a one-room schoolhouse.

Guevara had been defeated, but he remained defiant. When a guard spit in his face, Guevara spit back despite being tied up. He then kicked the soldier, causing him to double over in pain. Later, when other soldiers asked Guevara what he was thinking, he answered bravely, "I'm thinking about the immortality of the revolution, so feared by those you serve."[94]

While Guevara was lying bound in the schoolhouse, his fate was being decided by Bolivian officials. Although Prado's superiors had originally told him to keep Guevara alive, at 11:30 P.M. Barrientos issued an order to kill him. Historians claim Barrientos ordered Guevara's death to avoid a public trial, which Guevara could have used to rally opposition against his regime.

Che Impresses His Captor

"Che had an imposing look about him: clear eyes, a mane of hair that was almost red, and a thick, heavy beard. He wore a black beret, a filthy military uniform, and a blue jacket with a hood; he was almost bare-chested, as his tunic had no buttons on it."

Bolivian army captain Gary Prado, quoted in Paco Ignacio Taibo II, *Guevara, Also Known as Che*. New York: St. Martin's, 1997, p. 551.

Early the next day, a helicopter arrived with several high-ranking army officers and CIA agent Félix Rodríguez. A Cuban who had fled to the United States when Castro seized power, Rodríguez hated Communists and was not impressed with the captive: "He was a wreck. His clothes were filthy, ripped in several places and missing most of their buttons. He didn't have proper shoes, only pieces of leather wrapped around his feet and tied with cord."[95] Rodriguez took pictures of Guevara and of documents he had, including his diary.

One of the last photographs ever taken of Guevara shows the revolutionary with his mule, Chico, in late September 1967.

Rodríguez tried to persuade the soldiers to let Guevara live, because U.S. officials wanted to question him about his revolutionary activities. The Bolivian officers refused and asked for a volunteer to execute Guevara. Sergeant Mario Terán volunteered. At 1:10 P.M., Terán walked into the schoolhouse. Terán later claimed that Guevara looked at him and said, "I know you are here to kill me. Shoot, coward, you are only going to kill a man."[96]

Terán had been ordered to make it look like Guevara had been killed in battle. He shot Guevara several times in the legs, but he remained alive. With Guevara biting his wrist to keep from screaming in agony at his wounds, Terán shot him in the chest. The thirty-nine-year-old Guevara died as his lungs filled with blood.

The Strange Fate of Guevara's Body

That afternoon, soldiers tied Guevara's body to the skids of a helicopter and flew him to Vallegrande, a larger community about 20 miles (30km) away. In Vallegrande, Guevara's corpse was taken to a hospital, where his body was washed and he was shaved so that he would be recognizable to reporters who had assembled for a news conference. The body was put on public display in the hospital laundry room. All that night and into the next day, journalists, hospital staff, and local residents came to see Guevara's corpse.

Many of those who came to gawk at the famed revolutionary were amazed at how peaceful he looked. "It was like he wasn't dead," said one man. "He was laid out on the stretcher with his

Was There a Curse on Che's Killers?

Many biographies about Che Guevara detail what happened afterward to people who played a role in his execution. Because many of them met violent deaths or had other misfortunes, some people claimed there was a curse on those who killed Guevara. Bolivian dictator René Barrientos, who ordered his execution, died in a helicopter crash in April 1969. Captain Gary Prado, who helped capture Guevara, was shot and paralyzed from the waist down in 1981 while trying to quell an armed revolt. Mario Terán, who killed Guevara, lived in terror for many years afterward because he feared someone would execute him for killing Guevara. Strangest of all, perhaps, was the fate of Félix Rodriguez, who worked for the U.S. Central Intelligence Agency. A quarter-century later, Rodriguez wrote about what he experienced shortly after Guevara was killed:

> As I walked in the cool mountain air I realized that I was wheezing, and that it was becoming hard to breathe. Che may have been dead but somehow his asthma—a condition I had never had in my life—had attached itself to me. To this day, my chronic shortness of breath is a constant reminder of Che.

Quoted in Jon Lee Anderson, *Che Guevara: A Revolutionary Life.* New York: Grove, 1997, p. 741.

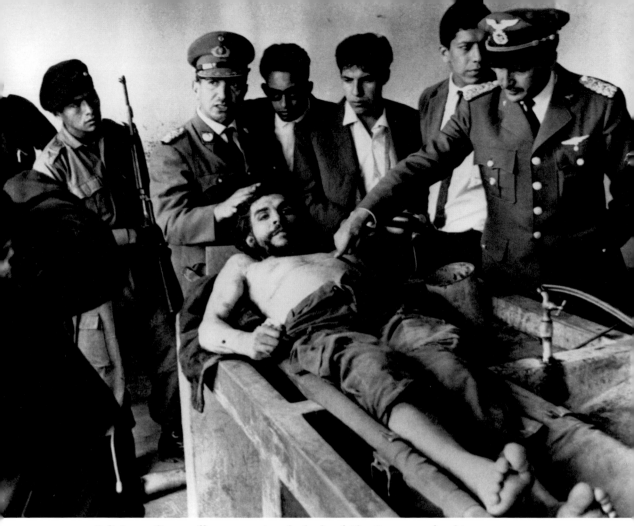

Bolivian military officers examine the body of Che Guevara after his execution. His body was put on public display to prove that he had been killed.

eyes open, looking at us, as if he was still alive."[97] Officials allowed photographers to take pictures of Guevara to prove to the world that he was dead. The shots of the bare-chested Guevara, his arms lying at his sides as if he were sleeping, were printed in newspapers around the world and became some of the most famous ever taken of him. The stories that accompanied the pictures claimed Guevara had died during combat.

On the night of October 10, Bolivian officials cut off Guevara's hands. They wanted his fingerprints checked one more time to ensure a positive identification. Rather than sending the body to a lab, however, they decided to just send his hands. Then they took his body to a secluded spot near the Vallegrande airport and buried Guevara and six of his comrades. Because officials did not want people to come to his grave to honor him, they claimed they had cremated his body and scattered his ashes in an unknown place.

In 1995, Bolivian general Mario Vargas Salinas decided to tell the truth about what had happened. He even revealed where Guevara's body was buried. Although it would take two more years, his body was dug up and returned to Cuba, and on October 17, 1997, Guevara was reburied in Santa Clara, the site of his most famous military victory. In a ceremony attended by Guevara's widow, Aleida March, and their children, Castro said Guevara was still an inspiration to revolutionaries around the world: "Che is fighting and winning more battles than ever. Thank you, Che, for your history, your life and your example. Thank you for coming to reinforce us in the difficult struggle in which we are engaged today to preserve the ideas for which you fought so hard."[98]

A Message for His Children

Before Guevara left for Bolivia, he had written a letter to his children that was to be read to them if he was killed. Signed simply "Papa," this final message expressed his love for his children. It also contained the wish he had for their future, one that summed up the guiding principle of Guevara's life: "Grow as good revolutionaries [and] remember that the revolution is the important thing and that each of us alone is worth nothing. Above all, always be capable of feeling most deeply any injustice committed against anyone, anywhere in the world. This is the most beautiful quality for a revolutionary."[99]

From Failed Revolutionary to Cultural Icon

Only three days after Che Guevara was executed, Thomas Hughes, a Latin America specialist for the U.S. State Department, sent secretary of state Dean Rusk a report that tried to explain what Guevara's death meant for the future. Hughes said the execution would cripple attempts for revolution in Bolivia and weaken future attempts by Fidel Castro to spread communism in Latin America. But Hughes also predicted that "Guevara will be eulogized as the model revolutionary who met a heroic death."[100] Castro brought that prophecy to life on October 18, 1967, when he delivered a eulogy for Guevara in Havana's Plaza de la Revolución.

In a lengthy speech before a crowd of almost a million people, Castro praised Guevara for having helped the Cuban Revolution succeed. To honor Guevara, he declared that October 8—the date of Guevara's last battle in Bolivia—would be celebrated annually as the "Day of the Heroic Guerrilla." Castro said Cubans should adopt Guevara as a role model because he embodied courage, self-sacrifice, and other qualities: "If we wish to express what we expect of our revolutionary combatants, our militants, our men to be, we must say, without hesitation: 'Let them be like Che!'"[101]

In the four decades since his death, many Cubans have tried to follow Castro's suggestion by working hard to make Cuba a better place to live, which had been Che's main goal in bringing revolution to Cuba. Surprisingly, Guevara also became—and remains today—a cultural hero to people in other nations, including the United States.

Che as Cultural Icon

That Guevara is still revered as a revolutionary decades after he died amazes many people. The Communist form of government he championed has now withered away. Even former Soviet countries have abandoned it, because its economic policies were failures and its governing style brutally denied people personal freedom. And critics like historian Alvaro Vargas Llosa, who bitingly refers to Guevara as the man "who did so much (or was it so little?) to destroy capitalism,"[102] point out that Guevara had more failures than successes. Guevara helped win the Cuban Revolution, but his economic policies hurt Cuba's economy, and his attempts to ignite revolution in the Congo and Bolivia flopped.

Biographer Jorge G. Castañeda believes Guevara's good looks, personal charisma, willingness to die for a cause he believed in, and the dramatic nature of his death combined to transform him into a romantic, powerful symbol of revolution despite those failures. Castañeda said Guevara became a hero to young people worldwide who were involved in social rebellion in the 1960s. This was especially true in the United States, where many tried to stop the Vietnam War, a conflict that Guevara also opposed. Said Castañeda: "He became the symbol of a generation, the symbol of a time, the 1960s, when young people tried to change the world as they thought best." Castañeda claims Guevara remains popular today because the social revolt he became identified with still exists: "[That] cultural rebellion is still with us today [and so] today he reappears as a symbol, not of the politics of the '60s, but of the cultural revolt of the '60s. That rebellion achieved enormous changes in society that are still with us today."[103]

Although Guevara's status as a cultural icon has continued to grow, he is treated today more as a popular celebrity, like a singer or an actor, rather than as a political revolutionary. The

Photographer Alberto Korda stands in front of the famous image of Che Guevara he captured in 1960.

result is that people buy merchandise emblazoned with the image of a man they know little about. A saying among young Latin Americans sums this up: "Tengo una remera del Che y no sé por qué," which in English means "I have a Che T-shirt and I don't know why."[104] An even more bitter irony is that the likeness of Guevara, who rejected capitalism, is helping companies that produce such items make money.

On an Internet site known as the CheStore, people can buy shirts, watches, and coffee mugs bearing Guevara's image, most of them from a photograph Alberto Korda took in 1960. The dramatic close-up of the bearded, long-haired Guevara, his beret set at a rakish angle as he stares intensely straight ahead, has been reproduced so often that it is one of the most famous pictures from the 1960s. His face has been plastered on the sides of buildings in Cuba and Latin America, printed on posters that have hung on the walls of countless college dormitory rooms, and even used in a vodka advertising campaign in Great Britain.

Guevara's cultural popularity was boosted in 2004 with the release of *The Motorcycle Diaries*, a movie about his early travels through Latin America. And it is in those countries that Guevara is more revered than anywhere else because he tried to help his fellow Latin Americans achieve a better life.

A Hero in Latin America

Ariel Dorfman is a human rights activist and professor of Latin American studies at Duke University in North Carolina. When he was a young man in Chile, Guevara's death angered Dorfman and other Latin Americans because they believed he was trying to make life better for poor people. Admitting that Guevara was "already a legend to my generation," Dorfman claims that he and others took to the streets in protest, shouting, "'No lo vamos a olvidar!' We won't let him be forgotten."[105]

Many Latin Americans still honor Guevara today. People from countries such as Argentina, Chile, Bolivia, and Colombia are among the more than two hundred thousand people who annu-

Many Latin Americans today consider Che Guevara a hero, even in La Higuera, Bolivia, where he was executed. Here, celebrants in La Higuera honor his memory during the thirtieth anniversary of Che Guevara's death.

ally visit his memorial in Santa Clara, Cuba. The monument includes a bronze sculpture 22.3 feet (6.8m) tall that portrays Guevara garbed as a guerrilla and holding a gun, with his asthma inhaler visible in a pocket.

In rural parts of Latin America, some people consider the dead revolutionary a saint. Strangely, one of the places he is most revered is La Higuera, the place where he died. Giovanni Osinaga, a doctor whose clinic is in the schoolhouse where Guevara was executed, says local residents pray to Guevara: "They ask him to bring rain, improve crop yield, or perform a miracle."[106] Guevara does provide one tangible benefit to the small village—tourists who spend money locally when they come to see where he was killed.

"A Girl Like Che"

Not all Hispanics admire Guevara. Teresa Dovalpage was born in Havana in 1966 and taught literature at the University of Havana before coming to the United States in 1996. Her 2004 novel, *A Girl Like Che Guevara*, is about a sixteen-year-old girl growing up in Cuba who hates communism, a sentiment the author shared with her main character. In an article in *Hispanic* magazine, Dovalpage wrote: "'We Pioneers want communism. We'll be like Che.' Until I was 15 years old, that was the slogan I repeated every morning at school, before the beginning of classes. I didn't really want to 'be like Che' and now I suspect many of my classmates didn't either, but we had to shout it at the top of our lungs."[107]

Although Dovalpage was not a fan of Guevara, she soon found out how many people still admire him. After the story was published in October 2004, Dovalpage received hate mail from people who revered Guevara. "Ay, ay ay, I didn't know Che Guevara still had so many followers here [in the United States]!"[108] she said in an interview about the rabid reaction to her book.

The emotional response Dovalpage experienced is typical of the intense feelings many people still have for Guevara. Thus a man who endured a lonely death in a jungle many years ago has achieved a kind of immortality and will probably never be forgotten.

Notes

Introduction: A "Complete Human Being"

1. Quoted in David Kunzle, "Seeing Che as Icon Through Artists' Eyes," UCLA Today. www.today.ucla.edu/1997/971010SeeingChe.html.
2. Quoted in Leo Sauvage, *Che Guevara: The Failure of a Revolutionary.* Englewood Cliffs, NJ: Prentice Hall, 1973, p. 115.
3. Quoted in Tad Szulc, *Fidel: A Critical Portrait.* New York: William Morrow, 1986, p. 596.
4. Andrew Sinclair, *Che Guevara.* New York: Viking, 1970, p. 107.

Chapter 1: Growing Up in Argentina

5. Quoted in Paco Ignacio Taibo II, *Guevara, Also Known as Che.* New York: St. Martin's, 1997, p. 10.
6. Quoted in I. Lavretsky, *Ernesto Che Guevara.* Moscow, Russia: Moscow Progress, 1976. www.chehasta.narod.ru/1stpart.html.
7. Quoted in Taibo II, *Guevara, Also Known as Che*, p. 4.
8. Quoted in Jorge G. Castañeda, *Compañero: The Life and Death of Che Guevara.* New York: Knopf, 1997, p. 8.
9. Quoted in Taibo II, *Guevara, Also Known as Che*, p. 9.
10. Quoted in Lavretsky, *Ernesto Che Guevara.*
11. Quoted in Taibo II, *Guevara, Also Known as Che*, p. 7.
12. Quoted in Public Broadcasting Corporation, "American Experience: Fidel Castro." www.pbs.org/wgbh/amex/castro/peopleevents/p_guevara.html.
13. Quoted in John Gerassi, ed., *Venceremos! The Speeches and Writings of Ernesto Che Guevara.* New York: Macmillan, 1968, p. 5.
14. Quoted in Taibo II, *Guevara, Also Known as Che*, p. 10.
15. Quoted in Martin Ebon, *Che: The Making of a Legend.* New York: Universe, 1969, p. 15.
16. Quoted in Castañeda, *Compañero*, p. 58.
17. Quoted in Gerassi, *Venceremos!* p. 7.

18. Quoted in Jon Lee Anderson, *Che Guevara: A Revolutionary Life.* New York: Grove, 1997, p. 63.
19. Quoted in Castañeda, *Compañero,* p. 36.

Chapter 2: Ernesto Guevara Becomes the Revolutionary Che

20. Quoted in Lavretsky, *Ernesto Che Guevara.*
21. Ernesto "Che" Guevara, *The Motorcycle Diaries: Notes on a Latin American Journey.* New York: Ocean, 2004, p. 39.
22. Quoted in Che Guevara, *Reminiscences of the Cuban Revolutionary War.* New York: Grove, 1968, p. 11.
23. Guevara, *The Motorcycle Diaries,* p. 63.
24. Quoted in Taibo II, *Guevara, Also Known as Che,* p. 21.
25. Quoted in Anderson, *Che Guevara,* p. 84.
26. Quoted in Castañeda, *Compañero,* p. 54.
27. Guevara, *The Motorcycle Diaries,* p. 32.
28. Quoted in Sinclair, *Che Guevara,* p. 5.
29. Quoted in Szulc, *Fidel,* p. 332.
30. Quoted in Taibo II, *Guevara, Also Known as Che,* p. 35.
31. Hilda Gadea, *Ernesto: A Memoir of Che Guevara.* Garden City, NY: Doubleday, 1972, p. 26.
32. Quoted in Ebon, *Che,* p. 32.
33. Quoted in Gerassi, *Venceremos!* p. 11.
34. Quoted in Anderson, *Che Guevara,* p. 165.
35. Quoted in Lavretsky, *Ernesto Che Guevara.*
36. Quoted in Castañeda, *Compañero,* p. 84.
37. Gadea, *Ernesto,* p. 54.
38. Quoted in History of Cuba, "Castro Talks About Che." www.historyofcuba.com/history/castro2.html.

Chapter 3: Che Helps Bring Revolution to Cuba

39. Quoted in Gadea, *Ernesto,* p. 126.
40. Quoted in Castañeda, *Compañero,* p. 90.
41. Quoted in Ebon, *Che,* p. 35.
42. Guevara, *Reminiscences of the Cuban Revolutionary War,* p. 44.
43. Quoted in Jackie K. Clark, "Che Guevara: Fundamentals of Guerrilla Warfare," GlobalSecurity.org. www.globalsecurity.org/military/library/report/1988/CJK.html.
44. Quoted in Castañeda, *Compañero,* p. 105.

G.R.C. Library

45. Quoted in *The Militant*, "I Argued That Women Too Could Fight," February, 19, 1996. www.themilitant.com/1996/607/607_30.html.

46. Steve Lewis, "Che Guevara and Guerilla Warfare, *Military Review*, September–October, 2001, p. 99.

47. Guevara, *Reminiscences of the Cuban Revolutionary War*, pp. 117–18.

48. Quoted in Anderson, *Che Guevara*, p. 251.

49. Quoted in Castañeda, *Compañero*, p. 105.

50. Quoted in Clark, "Che Guevara."

51. Quoted in Sinclair, *Che Guevara*, p. 42.

52. Guevara, *Reminiscences of the Cuban Revolutionary War*, p. 253.

53. Quoted in Taibo II, *Guevara, Also Known as Che*, p. 256.

Chapter 4: Che: A Man of Many Titles

54. Quoted in Taibo II, *Guevara, Also Known as Che*, p. 265.

55. Quoted in Alvaro Vargas Llosa, "The Killing Machine," *New Republic*, July 11, 2005, p. 28.

56. Manuel Piñeiro, *Che Guevara and the Latin American Revolutionary Movements*. Melbourne, Australia: Ocean, 2001, p. 49.

57. Quoted in Anderson, *Che Guevara*, p. 375.

58. Quoted in Taibo II, *Guevara, Also Known as Che*, p. 272.

59. Quoted in Herbert L. Matthews, *Fidel Castro*. New York: Simon and Schuster, 1969, p. 166.

60. Sinclair, *Che Guevara*, p. 50.

61. Quoted in Lavretsky, *Ernesto Che Guevara*.

62. Guevara, *Reminiscences of the Cuban Revolutionary War*, p. 276.

63. Quoted in Gerassi, *Venceremos!* p. 18.

64. Quoted in Taibo II, *Guevara, Also Known as Che*, p. 339.

65. Quoted in Sauvage, *Che Guevara*, p. 135.

66. CIA, "The Fall of Che Guevara and the Changing Face of the Cuban Revolution," Declassified National Security Archive. www.gwu.edu/~nsarchiv/NSAEBB/NSAEBB5/#books.

67. Quoted in Castañeda, *Compañero*, p. 317.

68. Quoted in Taibo II, *Guevara, Also Known as Che*, p. 283.

69. Quoted in Ebon, *Che*, p. 50.
70. Ernesto Guevara, *Che Guevara Speaks: Selected Speeches and Writings*. New York: Merit, 1967, p. 99.
71. Guevara, *Che Guevara Speaks*, p. 102.

Chapter 5: Failure in Africa

72. Quoted in Castañeda, *Compañero*, p. 141.
73. Quoted in Taibo II, *Guevara, Also Known as Che*, p. 408.
74. Guevara, *Che Guevara Speaks*, p. 108.
75. Quoted in Llosa, "The Killing Machine," p. 29.
76. Guevara, *Che Guevara Speaks*, p. 102.
77. Quoted in Anderson, *Che Guevara*, p. 637.
78. Guevara, *Che Guevara Speaks*, p. 140.
79. Ernesto Guevara, *The African Dream: The Diaries of the Revolutionary War in the Congo*. New York: Grove, 2000, p. 125.
80. Quoted in Castañeda, *Compañero*, p. 308.
81. Quoted in Ebon, *Che*, p. 68.
82. Guevara, *The African Dream*, p. 207.
83. Quoted in Castañeda, *Compañero*, p. 316.
84. Guevara, *Reminiscences of the Cuban Revolutionary War*, p. 267.

Chapter 6: Failure and Death in Bolivia

85. Guevara, *Che Guevara Speaks*, p. 142.
86. Piñeiro, *Che Guevara and the Latin American Revolutionary Movements*, p. 14.
87. Quoted in Ebon, *Che*, p. 95.
88. Ernesto Che Guevara, *The Bolivian Diary of Ernesto Che Guevara*. New York: Pathfinder, 1994, p. 102.
89. Quoted in Sauvage, *Che Guevara*, p. 157.
90. Quoted in Peter Kornbluh, "The Death of Che Guevara," Declassified National Security Archive. www.gwu.edu/~nsarchiv/NSAEBB/NSAEBB5/#chron.
91. Guevara, *The Bolivian Diary of Ernesto Che Guevara*, p. 253.
92. Guevara, *The Bolivian Diary of Ernesto Che Guevara*, p. 295.
93. Quoted in Castañeda, *Compañero*, p. 399.
94. Quoted in Taibo II, *Guevara, Also Known as Che*, p. 557.
95. Quoted in Gordon Ho McCormick, "The Legacy of a

Revolutionary Man," *World Policy Journal*, Winter 1997/98, p. 78.

96. Quoted in Anderson, *Che Guevara*, p. 739.

97. Quoted in Taibo II, *Guevara, Also Known as Che*, p. 564.

98. Quoted in Larry Rohter, "Cuba Buries Che, the Man, but Keeps the Myth Alive," *New York Times*, October 17, 1997, p. 1A.

99. Quoted in Gadea, *Ernesto*, p. 182.

Epilogue: From Failed Revolutionary to Cultural Icon

100. Thomas Hughes, "Guevara's Death—the Meaning for Latin America," Declassified National Security Archive. www.gwu.edu/~nsarchiv/NSAEBB/NSAEBB5/.

101. Quoted in Gerassi, *Venceremos!* p. 441.

102. Quoted in Llosa, "The Killing Machine," p. 25.

103. Quoted in Common Ground, "The Life of Che." www.commongroundradio.org/shows/97/9742.html.

104. Quoted in Llosa, "The Killing Machine," p. 29.

105. Ariel Dorfman, "Time 100: The Guerrilla Che Guevara," *Time*, June 14, 1999, p. 46.

106. Quoted in Jack Epstein, "Tiny Village Hopes Che Will Live on for Tourists," *Christian Science Monitor*, July 14, 1997, p. 7.

107. Teresa Dovalpage, "Why Che?" *Hispanic*, October 2005, p. 80.

108. Quoted in BellaOnline: The Voice of Women, "Author Q & A with Teresa de la Caridad Dovalpage," www.bellaon line.com/articles/art10778.asp.

Important Dates

1928
Ernesto Guevara de la Serna (later known as Che Guevara) is born in Rosario, Argentina.

1952
Guevara leaves on a ten-month tour of Latin America that also takes him to the United States.

1953
Guevara graduates as a doctor from the University of Buenos Aires.

1955
Guevara meets Fidel Castro and joins his effort to win control of Cuba.

1956
Guevara and eighty-one other men leave Tuxpan, Mexico, for Cuba on the small ship *Granma;* Guevara is wounded during an invasion of Las Coloradas in Cuba's Oriente Province.

1959
Cuban dictator Fulgencio Batista flees Cuba; Fidel Castro takes control of the country and grants Cuban citizenship to Guevara.

1964
Guevara travels to New York to speak at the United Nations and then embarks on a three-month diplomatic tour of Europe, Asia, and Africa.

1965
Guevara delivers a farewell letter to Castro and leaves for the Congo in Africa, where he will attempt to lead a revolution.

1966
Guevara arrives in Bolivia with hopes of overthrowing the government of General René Barrientos.

1967
Guevara is captured and executed in La Higuera, Bolivia.

1997
Guevara's body is exhumed and buried in Cuba.

2004
The movie *The Motorcycle Diaries*, based on Guevara's book by the same name, is released in theaters around the world.

For More Information

Books

David Downing, *Che Guevara*. Chicago: Heinemann, 2003. An informative biography for younger readers, including photos and maps.

Ernesto Guevara, *Che Guevara Reader: Writings by Ernesto Che Guevara on Guerrilla Strategy, Politics and Revolution*. New York: Ocean, 1997. A compilation of articles, speeches, and other material by Guevara.

Kate Havelin, *Che Guevara*. Minneapolis: Library Twenty-First Century, 2006. A solid biography of Guevara for younger readers.

Calvin Craig Miller, *Che Guevara: In Search of Revolution*. Greensboro, NC: Morgan Reynolds, 2006. A biography that thoroughly explains Guevara's life.

Anne E. Neimark, *Che! Latin America's Legendary Guerilla Leader*. New York: Lippincott, 1989. A biography of Che Guevara.

Harry Villegas (Pombo), *Pombo: With Che Guevara in Bolivia, 1966–68*. New York: Pathfinder, 1997. One of the Cuban soldiers Guevara led explains what happened in Bolivia.

Film

The Motorcycle Diaries. DVD. Directed by Walter Salles. Hollywood, CA: Universal Studios, 2004. A filmed version of Che Guevara's diary about his journey through Latin America with his friend Alberto Granado.

Web Sites

The Che Guevara Information Archive (www.geocities.com/ Hollywood/8702/che.html). This site includes a wide variety of information on Che Guevara, including links to many newspaper and magazine articles.

Che Guevara (www.chehasta.narod.ru/menu2.html). A comprehensive site that includes electronic files of a biography of Guevara, his writings, a time line of his life, photographs and illustrations, and audio files of him speaking.

Che Lives (www.che-lives.com). An Internet site with a biography and articles about Che Guevara, electronic copies of his written works and speeches, and links to other sites.

The Che Store (www.thechestore.com). In addition to selling articles bearing Che Guevara's name and likeness, this Internet site has a biography, electronic copies of his written works and speeches, and other material on him.

History of Cuba (www.historyofcuba.com/main/contents. html). An Internet site on Cuban history that includes copies of speeches and biographical information on Che Guevara.

Santa Clara's Che Guevara Memorial and Museum (www. hellocuba.ca/itineraries/310Che_Memorial.html). Photographs and information on Guevara's burial site and museum honoring him in Santa Clara, Cuba.

Index

Picture Credits

Cover: © Hulton Archive/Getty Images
© AFP/Getty Images, 67, 68
AP Photo, 11, 28, 31, 55, 79
AP Photo/Andrew St. George, 38
AP Photo/Antonio Suarez, 90
AP Photo/Bolivia Embassy, 75
AP Photo/PHOTOPRESS-Bilderdienst, Zuerich, 69
© Alan Oxley/Hulton Archive/Getty Images, 53
© Alejandro Ernesto/epa/Corbis, 21
© Arne Hodalic/Corbis, 56
© Bettmann/Corbis, 8, 41, 74, 83, 85
Canadien Press, 72
Canadien Press Photo/Cuban Archives, 15
© Claudia Daut/Reuters/Corbis, 46
© Craig Lovell/Corbis, 16
Film Four/South Fork/Senator Film/The Kobal Collection, 24, 29
© Hulton Archive/Getty Images, 35, 45, 62
© Jan Butchofsky-Houser/Corbis, 7
Maury Aaseng, 19
© Reuters/Corbis, 89
© Stephen Ferry/Getty Images, 37
© Time & Life Pictures/Getty Images, 49, 59

About the Author

Michael V. Uschan has written more than fifty books, including *Life of an American Soldier in Iraq*, for which he won the 2005 Council for Wisconsin Writers Juvenile Nonfiction Award. It was the second time he won the award. Mr. Uschan began his career as a writer and editor with United Press International, a wire service that provides stories to newspapers, radio, and television. As journalism is sometimes called "history in a hurry," Mr. Uschan considers writing history books a natural extension of the skills he developed in his many years as a journalist. He and his wife, Barbara, reside in the Milwaukee suburb of Franklin, Wisconsin.